ROSES FOR SOUTHERN GARDENS

ROSES

FOR SOUTHERN GARDENS

BY

BESSIE MARY BAIRD

Drawings by

CLIFFORD H. BALDOWSKI

Chapel Hill

THE UNIVERSITY

of North Carolina

PRESS

FOREWORD

THE NEED for specific information regarding varieties of ornamental plants best adapted to the South is great. So truly does this statement apply to roses that the reading of the manuscript of this book was a matter of genuine satisfaction to me.

Many of the new roses which have been introduced by various nurseries during the past two decades are unbelievably beautiful. One outstanding characteristic has been the development of subtly brilliant colors that the world has never before been privileged to enjoy. Descriptions in modern rose catalogues sound so remarkable that the average person is not inclined to take them seriously until he has actually seen some of the shadings of yellow, orange, copper, or salmon, pink, old rose, crimson, etc., or combinations of two or more of these yellow and pink tones. Another quality of our present-day Hybrid Tea which was not possessed by its ancestors in our grandparents' time is its form, particularly after it is past the bud stage.

To visit the garden of the author and see specimens of modern climbers, standards, bush Hybrid Teas, and Floribundas; or attend a Garden Club function at the Old Medical College in Augusta and see roses in silver bowls where full-blown and half-blown blooms and perfect, pointed buds have been used together in the same exquisite arrangement is indeed a treat. Such an experience has convinced many a gardener that modern roses have far more to offer in intrinsic beauty than the older varieties.

Not all of the roses listed in modern catalogues are

adapted to the Southeast. This timely treatise deals with the author's first-hand knowledge gained in the development of her own garden over a period of years. Her notes regarding varieties which have succeeded or failed, the general culture of the modern rose, and lists of favorites in various sections of the South are a real contribution to garden literature. It has been said that to be successful, gardening must be tranquil. The sound, practical advice offered in this testimonial on growing roses will help beginners gain the self-assurance for their endeavors which is a prerequisite to tranquillity and will inevitably direct them to lovelier ends.

Hubert B. Owens

Landscape Architecture Department
University of Georgia
Athens, Georgia

ACKNOWLEDGMENTS

For such a slender volume I am indebted to a great many friends:

To William Groat, of the Augusta, Georgia, Book Store, whose idea it was in the first place that I should write this book.

To Hubert B. Owens, Head of the Department of Landscape Architecture, University of Georgia, who has graciously written the Foreword. His interest in the completion of this book kept my courage to the sticking point.

To the members of my "Board of Experts":
Clyde and Ramona Stocking, Rose Growers, San Jose, California, who have steadily coached me from the sidelines ever since I planted my first rose bush. They have not only shared the wealth of their knowledge and experience with me and answered multitudinous questions via airmail, but have painstakingly checked this manuscript. The name Stocking is a synonym for Rose in my vocabulary.

Eugene S. Boerner, Head Hybridizer of Jackson & Perkins Company, and Roberta Lord of Conard-Pyle Company, who kindly read this manuscript and offered many helpful suggestions.

Dr. L. M. Massey of Cornell University, who contributed valuable information on spraying; and Professors W. O. Collins and Joel Giddens of the University of Georgia, who gave practical advice on fertilizing and the pH of the soil.

My sincere thanks are also extended to Archibald Rutledge, Hampton Plantation, McClellanville, South Carolina, for permission to quote his method of handling roots; and to the following nurseries for the generous loan of color plates:

Armstrong Nurseries (Ontario, California) for Charlotte Armstrong and Forty-Niner

The Conard-Pyle Company (West Grove, Pennsylvania) for Peace, Mme. Henri Guillot, and Mme. Cochet-Cochet

Jackson & Perkins Company (Newark, N. Y.) for Crimson Glory, Eclipse, and Countess Vandal

As Alice in Wonderland said, "What is the use of a book without pictures or conversations?" I am deeply grateful to Clifford H. Baldowski for his enthusiastic portrayal of the Lady Gardener, Sim, and the Roses, and to my twenty-eight Rose Poll contributors for the "conversations" which prevent this book from being a monologue.

Bessie Mary Baird

Augusta, Georgia
November, 1948

CONTENTS

Contents   xi

LIST OF COLOR PLATES

A NOTE ON THE COLOR PLATES

To the charge of unfairness in including in this art gallery the spectacular All-American winner, Forty-Niner, and omitting color plates of Rose Poll winners, Etoile de Hollande, Editor McFarland, and Picture, the defense points out that there are no flattering portraits of these varieties too old to be patented. To my complaint to Conard-Pyle that the likeness of Mme. Henri Guillot fails to do her justice, Roberta Lord of that firm readily agreed, declaring that many a rose could win a suit for misfeasance because of pictures published in catalogues. A suggestion to you novices selecting your first roses: If you run across a rose labeled "Picture," don't be discouraged. Turn the page and find the open bloom of Floribunda Rosenelfe, magnify it in your mind's eye, but in a soft shade of all-over, not two-toned, pink, and then you will have a better picture of Picture.

On the other hand, a recent trend is to make as glamorous photographs of the newest rose introductions as of the latest Hollywood favorites. What could be more tantalizingly lovely than the poses in current catalogues of those California originations, Taffeta, Nocturne, and Show Girl? Heaven grant that these beauties prove easier to domesticate than the Hollywood starlets themselves.

ROSES FOR SOUTHERN GARDENS

By Way of Introduction

ROSES BELONG IN EVERY
SOUTHERN GARDEN

HAD THE REPUBLICANS not borrowed it some years back, any Southern politician would be proud to dust off old King Henry's slogan, take it to his bosom, and campaign for "A chicken in every pot in Dixie." I, myself, would favor such a platform, if only I might add another plank, boldly declaring for "Roses in the yard of every Southern home"—be it ever so humble. Man cannot live by bread alone, or even served up bountifully with fried chicken on the side. For the good of his esthetic soul, he needs the stimulus that only roses blooming in the spring can give. In this Southland of ours, there are varieties which cost so little in effort, but which return so much. There are roses for every yard.

May I say here, O small gardener of the South, that this light-hearted treatise is intended for you, a person who has long been overlooked in the voluminous bulk of American rose literature. So far all of the books seem written for a climate in the latitude of Connecticut, with a great deal of space allotted to arcticness and winter protection, and no mention made of summer care under the hot Southern sun. It was the late Dr. Nicolas, distinguished rosarian, who said, "Rome is an example where summer hardiness is more important than winter hardiness." In the present

1

instance, we Southerners find it wiser to do as the Romans, and not as the Yankees.

It is my hope that you who expect the maximum of bloom from the minimum of plants may find in this primer much sound and easily remembered advice.

↝ 1 ↜

ROSE GENEALOGY

(*Pocket Edition*)

M R. AND MRS. BEGINNER: In order that you may
acquire the proper background, may I present the
important families of the Rose Kingdom?

HYBRID PERPETUALS

Characteristics

Hardiness making for Northern popularity. Buxom
plants which go bare-legged in summer. Huge, fragrant
flowers which, holding their dead petals, do not age grace-
fully. Color range limited. No clear yellows.

Examples

1. Paul Neyron (lilac-rose), a Southern favorite of yester-
year.

2. Scentless Frau Karl Druschki (sometimes called White
American Beauty), the only variety extensively grown in the
South. Seeding and sprouting so admirably, the Frau has
become the Queen Victoria of the Royal Rose Family. This
"Great White Mother" is famous for her flamboyant Spanish
descendants.

TEAS

Characteristics

Adapted to moderate winters and hot, moist summers;
still much used along the Gulf Coast. Large, long-lived

3

plants, retentive of smooth, healthy foliage. Fragrant, refined bloom of good form, often hanging its head. Soft-textured petals, slow to open, sometimes "balling" or withering in the bud. Color range limited. No brilliant yellows.

HYBRID TEAS

Characteristics

Moderately vigorous plants. Recurrent blooming habit. Perfection of form. Usually moderate fragrance. Marvelous range of colors.

The Hybrid Tea, result of an original cross (Hybrid Perpetual x Tea), is the most valuable garden rose of today.

POLYANTHAS

Characteristics

Small flowers borne in clusters. The larger-flowered Hybrid Polyanthas are usually called Floribundas.

CLIMBERS

The parentage of climbers is highly involved. They are generally differentiated, from the Northern point of view, as hardy or tender; but this classification becomes academic in the lower and middle South, where all are hardy.

Characteristics: Hardy

Often producing excellent flowers on one-year-old wood. Popular over the entire United States. As a rule, spring bloomers only.

Examples: Hardy
1. Dr. Van Fleet
2. Paul's Scarlet

On the borderline of hardiness for the North, but perfectly safe for the upper South are Paul's Lemon Pillar, Mermaid, and such beauties from Australia as Daydream, Kitty Kininmonth, and Billy Boiler.

Characteristics: Tender

Producing best flowers on mature wood three or four years old. Although hybridizers are patiently developing hardy and sub-zero roses for the North, we in the South already have at hand a wealth of beautiful varieties to choose from.

Examples: Tender

1. Cherokee

2. Banksia.—Both Cherokee and Banksia are highly prized wild forms from China, now naturalized in the South. Both were planted in Empress Josephine's garden at Malmaison.

3. Climbing Tea.—"Sports" from the bush Teas. Almost indistinguishable from Noisettes.

4. Noisette.—Once famous for such celebrities as Lamarque and Maréchal Niel. Noisette originally started out in bush form (Pink Cluster) at Charleston, South Carolina.

5. Gigantea.—Belle of Portugal, chief Southern representative.

6. Climbing Polyantha.—Noteworthy only as climbing edition of Sweetheart Rose, at one time very popular with the gentlemen for boutonnières.

7. Climbing Hybrid Tea.—Principally "sports" from the bush varieties. Recurrent bloomers with a big future in the South.

Famous Ancestor in the Hybrid Tea Line

AUSTRIAN YELLOW

(The Fetid Rose). Brilliant yellow wild rose, parent of Persian Yellow.

Characteristics

Musky odor lacking fragrance. Rapid growth. Rapid opening of bloom. Clean dropping of petals. Glossy, short-lived foliage, very attractive on the bush but particularly subject to blackspot.

In 1900 Pernet-Ducher electrified the world with the first clear yellow garden rose (red Hybrid Perpetual x Persian Yellow). This strain, called at first Pernetiana, after countless crossings was absorbed by the Hybrid Tea line.

The Fetid Rose should not be looked upon as the skeleton in the Hybrid Tea closet, strongly injecting into the royal bloodstream that worse-than-hemophilia curse, blackspot, but rather as the giver of new life and color.

The results were revolutionary (see "Characteristics" above)—not only more abundant bloom but colors never before seen in the rose—clear, deep yellows, orange and copper blends, and flaming scarlets which do not fade or "blue."

Heredity among Roses

Within the same flower are pistils (female) and pollen-bearing stamens (male). In crosses, generally, the female provides the dominant characteristics of vegetation, form of flower, size of petals; the male provides color, to the second or third generation.

Some varieties are excellent as females, worthless as males, and vice versa. Often an interesting characteristic does not appear until the second or third generation.

๙ 2 ๖

THE QUEEN OF THE GARDEN

How Many Roses?

GROWING ROSES CAN BE FUN—provided you don't plant too many. Some people seem to think that success follows in direct proportion to the number of bushes they set out. Then, if their luck is only mediocre with one hundred, they enthusiastically make plans to add another hundred. Now I hold the theory that two or three dozen rose bushes, well loved and cared for personally, will yield more in quality bloom and satisfaction than ten times as many with hit-or-miss attention. Although I am never happier than when working with my roses, I want to feel that I own them, not that they own me.

Parting with Tradition

Does mention of a flower garden immediately bring to mind your grandmother's rose beds of geometric pattern, primly edged with box? Granted that is an alluring picture, do you still contend that your garden space is not sufficient for formal beds—and roses? Does, however, a picket fence as dividing line go marching down your yard, with an occasional tree or shrub to mark its progress? If so, you have the making of a lovely border. First, imagine roses climbing the entire length of the fence for background. Those three natural divisions, when widened, will become three separate

7

beds, which you can tie together in front with one continuous ribbon of identical edging. The very shady portion will do nicely for bleeding-heart and small azaleas, or columbine and violets. The hot sandy stretch in stark sunshine, where nandina roots will offer keen competition, was meant for bearded iris, but that broadly curving bed, which enjoys light shade a few hours in the early afternoon, is perfect for roses.

Other Flowers in the Rose Border

Can other flowers be grown judiciously in this rose bed in your border? I confess it is heresy, but my answer is "yes," because your exposure is sufficiently sunny. Don't forget, however, that your roses are your parlor boarders, paying big returns in the world's favorite bloom from late March and April to November and even early December. Chrysanthemums Mme. Chiang Kai-shek and Mrs. Pierre S. duPont III may enjoy the same sumptuous fare, but tolerate them at head table only so long as they do not elbow their betters and eat too heartily of the dishes prepared especially for the roses. As congenial companions, content to keep a polite distance, they contribute welcome shade during the intense heat of summer. Poor country cousin, Dwarf Petunia, may be invited in to serve as ground cover, not for Petunia's sake, but because she treads so lightly that she will keep the royal rose roots cool. When she ceases to act lowly, off with her head!

Tree roses * are ideal with other flowers. You will never regret their extravagance in the border if you offset the cost with one packet of miniature dahlia seed. These you will sow in a separate spot in March, moving the plants to their real home underneath the tree roses when the spring annuals and pansies are ready to be discarded. Even though these low-bedding dahlias tend to outgrow themselves in such good earth, do not stake them, but allow them—if need be—to hump along camel-wise, to furnish you with colorful

* See below, Chapter IV, "Standards."

bloom from July till frost. They will also serve as a water-gauge for the roses. Whenever the dahlias wilt, let the hose run at their feet, and you find that the roses, too, will profit from the moisture. Furthermore, the following spring you will have an earlier crop from the dahlia tubers that you lift and divide.

Another dovetailing combination is Sweet William and Spoon chrysanthemums. The Sweet William will have time to finish their act and take a curtain call with their side florets before pink and white Spoons demand all of the stage. Pinch back these finicky growers a couple of times to make them branch, stake and tie them inconspicuously, patiently disbud, and your border can hold its own fall festival. Although you may claim full credit for the splendor of the roses, you must surely admit that the fairies have had a hand with the Spoons. Moreover, these long-lasting beauties are equally decorative when brought indoors to share a bowl with the roses.

Never will you read in the Northern books how tree roses must be dug up for winter, or have their heads bent low under sackcloth and boughs, without feeling a touch of pride that yours remain erect all year, to queen it over a succession of subjects.

To add to the effect of unity in your border, you may group Daylily Hyperion and Star of Gold in each of your three beds. Liriope (*Muscari*) and her kinsman (usually called Ophiopogon), little fountains of foliage with blue spikes held high in midsummer, will solve in simplest manner your outer edging problem. Clipped back in the spring, when the new shoots are ready to appear, they will turn the footlights over to a row of candytuft behind them, at blooming time.

In the inner row of your triple edging, *Sedum spectabile* (liking sunshine and shade in the same undemanding fashion as his fellows), besides putting on a one-man show in September, will perform interestingly all season until snapped off for the winter. Then in February the small rosettes will creep out and begin again their life cycle.

For variety among these low growers, scalloped-leaved coral bells may be tucked into any reasonably moist nook, but, tell me, where can you find such a gal as blue-eyed *Plumbago larpentae* to bask happily in the sunshine, even on your hot terrace rocks, the summer long? Can't somebody find her a better name? She certainly deserves it!

3

CLIMBERS

Climbing Hybrid Teas

YOU WILL REMEMBER from your Rose Genealogy that many Hybrid Teas have "sported" into climbers, which, I am happy to say, are often healthier than the parent. There are Etoile de Hollande and Christopher Stone among the reds; Picture, a medium-sized, patrician pink; the matchless Mrs. Sam McGredy, and the newcomer, Mme. Henri Guillot, my pets among the bi-colors. After the marvelous spring display, there is often later bloom, Mrs. Sam McGredy being especially generous as a repeater. These climbers are nature's gift to the Southland. They demand only moderate pruning to keep them comely, bearing their best flowers on stems springing from the older wood. Given the same care as any Hybrid Tea, they will yield myriads of long-stemmed roses equal or superior to those grown on a bush.

You will want to start early to train their branches to grow low, bringing them back and forth on the fence and tying them as you go along, instead of twining them in and out of the palings. In this way you will not have to go after a step-ladder at cutting and dusting time, and you will not make such a scratchy business out of pruning. Moreover, the horizontal method will mean better flowers for you, with longer stems. Since botanists tell us that sunlight stimulates the production of flowers, it seems to me poor practice to bunch the canes of Hybrid Tea climbers, binding them tightly around a post, or a pipe which would become very hot in summer.

To be specific, if you expect your climbing Picture to live up to her reputation as a recurrent performer, stretch out her branches, spray (or dust) to keep them clothed with foliage, fertilize lightly but often, water copiously, and when the season is right Picture will repay you not only in the spring but again in the fall with a bower of bloom.

Climbers Requiring Little Care

A top-notcher among the large-flowered hardy climbers is the delicate-pink Dr. Van Fleet. This rose is delicate only in coloring, and needs practically no pruning or care. He will cheerfully play second fiddle on Mrs. Sam McGredy's fence in a shady spot, where a Hybrid Tea would sulk, and will regale you with a cadenza of spring bloom. Furthermore, New Dawn, an identical twin, possesses the ability to repeat. This pair will really go to town if you don't fence them in. Given the most inauspicious corner of your house, they will soon screen your verandah, or, clambering Heavenwards, make yours a rose-covered cottage such as one reads about in story books.

Rampant yellow Banksia, assigned to your garage, where she will have plenty of room, will shower it with a cascade of tiny double blossoms to usher in the spring. Although your friends who are confirmed rose addicts may build trellises and arbors, happily for you beginners, a tree and a climbing single rose have a natural affinity for each other. Any of your stately oaks or lofty pines will be honored to bear the attractive foliage and flowers of Silver Moon and primrose Mermaid; however, let pink Cherokee, with blue *Phlox divaricata* at her feet, be your first choice. Because Mermaid follows Cherokee and has the additional advantage of repeating intermittently in summer and fall, even the lazy gardeners among you may enjoy a succession of color.

Don't take Cherokee and Banksia for granted because in the lower and middle South they require little or no attention. If only these Southern beauties were hardy, they would be sitting for their portraits in all of the Northern catalogues.

♪ 4 ♪

STANDARDS

What Is a Standard?

O FTEN I ENCOUNTER CONFUSION in the public
mind as to exactly what a standard is. Now if you will
notify your nurseryman before May, he can insert two
"buds" of any variety you fancy in one end of a smooth
stem * (36-42 inches long) the other end of which he has
grafted on wild understock. The result will be a "full"
standard—in ordinary garden parlance, a tree rose—that is
to say, an eye-level rose bush growing lollipop fashion
on a tall stem. Upright President Hoover would look out
of balance precariously perched on such slender underpin-
ning; on the other hand, spreading varieties make an attractive, compact head. These aristocrats of the rose world
lend height and distinction to simple flower plantings as
well as to formal rose beds. They are space savers in the
border, for low plants may grow underneath the "tree."

Much less popular are half standards, budded 18-24 inches
from the ground. Floribundas are sometimes used effectively
at this level.

Low standards (8-10 inches) may be substituted for regu-
lar bush roses. They have the advantage in summer of not
being in close proximity to the hot earth, and of being easier

* Usually IXL in California, and a special *Multiflora japonica* in
Northern nurseries.

to water without wetting the foliage. As a result, they are husky growers.

Pernet-Ducher, the great hybridizer, was wont to remark, "Do not judge a rose until you see it on a standard."

Standards in the Border

A BI-COLOR BED

Why leave to the connoisseurs these spectacular standards which produce the finest bloom? Tree roses will fill your heart with pride if you choose four, or three, or even two of that superb variety, Mme. Henri Guillot, whose huge buds open to camellia-like flowers of rich raspberry, and whose foliage is distinctly handsome. If your first interest is the general garden picture and you want a bit of cream color for contrast, prolific Pedrálbes will make heads as rounded as an old-fashioned nosegay. Her fecundity will compensate for the fact that her limber-necked blossoms require a low bowl when made into an arrangement. Then behind these charming ladies, climbing Mrs. Sam McGredy, bless her, will do honor to your fence.

Spaced between the tree roses, either low standards or bush roses will soon look at home. Moderate growers such as Charlotte Armstrong and Mme. Cochet-Cochet are best; avoid leggy numbers like Texas Centennial, whose height here would detract, though excellent in the background.

If there is room out in front, a row of foot-high Margo Kosters, the darling of the Polyanthas, will add just the finishing touch. Because the blossoms remain cupped, they will make you think that elves frolicking all night in your garden have anchored to each branch many a tiny sheaf of coral balloons. These will furnish you with a ready-made corsage whenever you fare forth in your best finery, that is, in springtime and in autumn. Margo does not like hot weather, and will need in summer a little thinning out for ventilation.

A PINK BED

In case your preference runs to pinks, Sierra Glow or J. Otto Thilow will make effective standards, with Picture a splendid climber. President Macia and Sonata are my suggestions in the bush line. As for Polyanthas, there is a new one by the name of Pinkie, suitably low and compact, whose buds, although miniature, are perfect.

It is well to remind you here that most of the larger-flowered Hybrid Polyanthas, called Floribundas, grow tall, the popular Rosenelfe averaging three feet, and Betty Prior, four feet. Although many have attractive buds, these oftentimes turn blowsy when full open and, dry and crisp, hang on to spoil the beauty of the cluster. In the North, where their hardiness is an asset, Polyanthas and Floribundas are prized for mass color. Not usually a disappointment in the South if grouped in 3's to 6's, and if given the same protection against blackspot as the Hybrid Teas, they possess the virtue of permanence in the perennial border. If you will bury their dead for them, daily snipping off their withered flowers, Polyanthas and Floribundas will impart a fresh and colorful appearance to your garden.

A RED BED

In the family of reds you will discover as many permutations and combinations as you could wish. The faithful three, Etoile de Hollande, Christopher Stone, and Crimson Glory, will develop into good standards as well as bushes. Moreover, the climbing edition of Etoile is an old favorite; climbing Christopher is rapidly becoming known; and climbing Crimson Glory is sure to win friends now that she is out in trade. Incidentally, this trio is strong on perfume, outstripped only by scarlet San Fernando.

A RED-AND-YELLOW BED

A combination red-and-yellow bed can be stunning, when climber Sungold and Floribunda Goldilocks serve as foils for Crimson Glory standards. Although rose colors in the

Plant Pat. No. 591

PEACE
"Deservedly the most publicized Rose in the world"

garden rarely clash, you may well use your judgment in mixing them.

Low Standards: A Novelty
(8-10 Inch)

For the something-new-under-the-rose-sun you might try a low standard of Eclipse or Peace as a shrub at some strategic point in your garden. This novelty, if you are only a casual observer, is a regulation rose bush growing to fat-lady size.

Floriferous Eclipse is a "cropper"; pruned lightly after each flowering, she will flaunt an amazing quantity of golden blooms actually five or six times during the year. At her peak she resembles a miniature Christmas tree be-decked with lighted candles. I regret to say that her stream-lined buds sometimes turn into slatterns at maturity.

Many-petaled Peace, however, like The Doctor and Mme. Henri Guillot, is most beautiful when fully open. To me, roses have distinct personalities. Peace reminds me of a blonde circus performer, whose pink tights display her every curve to best advantage. Not only has a single perfect specimen more "oomph" than any camellia, but the two tones of rich cream and cerise make her a natural in a bowl of mixed flowers. For you small gardeners, who at times can pick only a handful of blossoms, this is a definite asset. Furthermore, an exciting counterpart exists in Gladiolus Corona, her spittin' image as to coloring. Truly no Southern garden is complete without Peace!

Care of Full Standards: (36-42 Inch)

Tree roses require a minimum of care in the South. At planting time use a half-inch iron stake, four and a half or five feet long (which may extend into the head). Select a Chinese bamboo pole, three or four inches in diameter; saw into pieces two or three inches shorter than the tree-rose stem. Then saw each division lengthwise and knock out the joints. Fit the two pieces together around the stem just below the crown, but on account of termites not reaching to the ground. Fasten together in two places with copper wire or friction tape, and again to the stake. The stake is best put on the outside of the casing.

The bamboo will afford needed protection against an occasional drop in the mercury below twenty degrees, and will also act as a summer shield to prevent intense sunshine from drawing sap out of the stem. A casing of the size suggested will allow the stem room enough in which to grow.

In the upper South in winter, it is customary to tie wheat straw around the head to protect the bud union, while allowing some circulation of air. "Duplex crinkled waterproof tree wrap" usually substitutes for bamboo canes.

⁓ 5 ⁓

PLANNING FORMAL ROSE BEDS

Two Simplified Versions

IF YOU WANT TO FOLLOW in Grandma's footsteps and let at least one of your rose beds go formal, sketched here are two simple rectangular plans that would surely have gained the dear old lady's approval. Such a bed is perfect when cut out of a lawn, which not only helps to absorb the heat and hold an even moisture but serves as a frame for the rose picture as well.

RECTANGULAR BED, 8 x 15 feet. Suggested color combinations:

1. Pink
   one J. Otto Thilow standard, and
   four J. Otto Thilow bushes (for center row)
   four Sonata or Sierra Glow bushes (on one side)
   four Picture or President Macia bushes (on other side)

2. Bi-color
   one Mme. Henri Guillot standard, and
   four Mme. Henri Guillot bushes (for center row)
   four Saturnia or Taffeta bushes (on one side)
   four Charlotte Armstrong bushes (on other side)

3. Yellow
   one Peace standard, and
   four Peace bushes (for center row)

four Eclipse bushes (on one side)
four Soeur Thérèse bushes (on other side)

RECTANGULAR BED, 8 x 21 feet. Suggested color combinations:

1. Pink

   three J. Otto Thilow standards (excellent heads)
   four J. Otto Thilow bushes, alternating with standards
   six Sonata or Sierra Glow bushes (on one side)
   six Picture or President Macia bushes (on other side)

2. Bi-color

   three Mme. Henri Guillot standards
   four Mme. Henri Guillot bushes, alternating with standards
   six Angels Mateu or Countess Vandal bushes (on one side)
   six Charlotte Armstrong bushes (on other side)

3. Yellow

   three Peace standards
   four Peace bushes, alternating with standards
   six Eclipse bushes (on one side)
   six Soeur Thérèse bushes (on other side)

   SUGGESTED GROUND COVER

1. Six-inch Lobelia in blue shades

2. Six-inch Virginia stock in rose, white, or mixed shades.

Annuals such as these are not much bother, sometimes reseed themselves, and do not take nourishment from the rose roots. Space has been allowed for your favorite edging.

RECTANGULAR BED 8 x 15 FT.

1 Standard Rose
12 Bush Roses

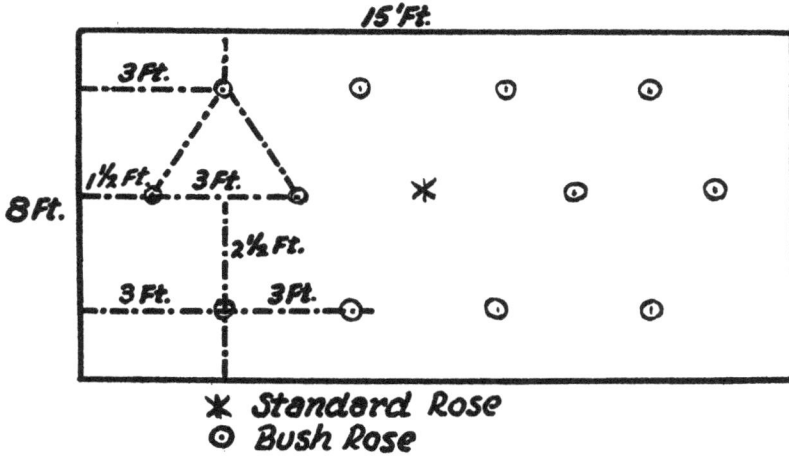

15'Ft.

3 Ft.

1½ Ft.   3 Ft.

8 Ft.

2½ Ft.

3 Ft.   3 Ft.

✳ *Standard Rose*
⊙ *Bush Rose*

RECTANGULAR BED 8 x 21 FT.

3 Standard Roses
16 Bush Roses

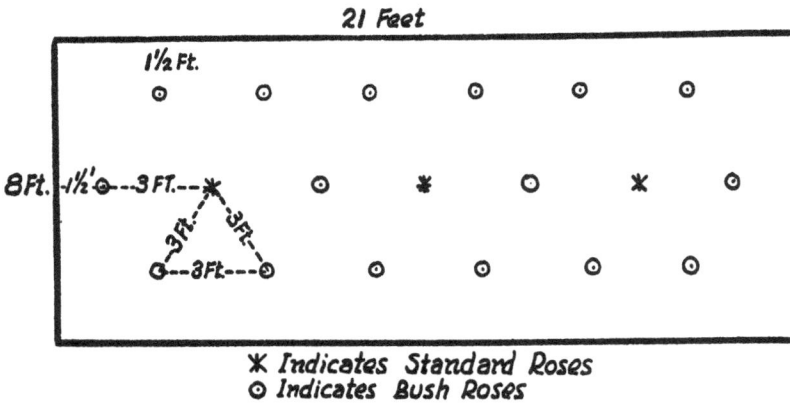

21 Feet

1½ Ft.

8 Ft. 1½' 3 FT.

3 Ft.   3 Ft.

3 Ft.

✳ *Indicates Standard Roses*
⊙ *Indicates Bush Roses*

Comparative Heights and Other Data

It is impossible to give the exact height of any variety, for roses perform differently in different locations.

TALL GROWERS

President Hoover	Katherine Marshall
Texas Centennial	Mrs. Edward Laxton
Susan Louise	Red Talisman
Girona	Radiances
Signora	Mrs. Charles Bell
Eclipse	Dainty Bess
Korovo	Rubaiyat
Peace	San Fernando
Ambassador	Forty-Niner
	New Yorker

MODERATE GROWERS

Crimson Glory	Charlotte Armstrong
Countess Vandal	Picture
Horace McFarland	Mme. Henri Guillot
Editor McFarland	Duchess of Peñaranda
Mme. Cochet-Cochet	Grande Duchesse Charlotte
Saturnia	Sonata
Sierra Glow	Hinrich Gaede
Etoile de Hollande	Taffeta
Faïence	Nocturne

LOW GROWERS

Christopher Stone	Fantasia
Mrs. Pierre S. duPont	Snowbird
Lulu	Fred Edmunds
Kaiserin Auguste Viktoria	Pedrálbes

TALL-GROWING FLORIBUNDAS

Floradora	Goldilocks
Pinocchio	Betty Prior
Red Ripples	Rosenelfe

LOW-GROWING POLYANTHAS AND FLORIBUNDAS

Perle d'Or	The Fairy
Cécile Brunner	Pinkie
Gruss an Aachen	Margo Koster

NEW VARIETIES SUITED TO THE SOUTH

Taffeta, beauteous offspring of Mrs. Sam McGredy and President Hoover.

San Fernando, excellent red which can stand sun. Intensely fragrant.

Nocturne, promising red. May burn a bit but does not blue.

High Noon, yellow pillar. Repeats.

Forty-Niner, vivid coloring, petals yellow outside, red inside.

Tallyho, a glorified Betty Uprichard. Stands the heat better than Forty-Niner.

Fashion, will set the style in Floribundas. As luscious as a ripe peach. Absolutely "tops." Available in fall, 1949.

STANDARDS, 36-42-inch,* SUGGESTED VARIETIES (Those of spreading habit are best adapted.)

Charlotte Armstrong	Christopher Stone
Crimson Glory	J. Otto Thilow
Fantasia	McGredy's Yellow
Mark Sullivan	Mrs. Pierre S. duPont
Mme. Henri Guillot	Pedrálbes
Saturnia	Snowbird
Sierra Glow	Sonata
The Chief	Peace (although a fairly tall
Picture	grower—produces superla-
Etoile de Hollande	tive bloom on a standard)

* Some nurseries prefer 36-inch and others 42-inch standards.

EXCELLENT HYBRID TEA CLIMBERS

Etoile de Hollande
Mme. Henri Guillot

Mrs. Sam McGredy
Picture
Sungold

VARIETIES FOR FULL SUN

Charlotte Armstrong
Sierra Glow
Peace
President Hoover
Talisman
Santa Anita
Red Ripples

San Fernando
Texas Centennial
Christopher Stone
President Macia
The Chief
Ambassador
Girona
Pinocchio

VARIETIES FOR PARTIAL SHADE (All prefer partial afternoon shade.)

Fantasia
Crimson Glory
Eclipse
Etoile de Hollande
Hinrich Gaede
Diane de Broglie
Lulu
Mark Sullivan

Nocturne
Mme. Henri Guillot
Mrs. Edward Laxton
Mrs. Pierre S. duPont
Shot Silk
Rapture
The Doctor
Peachblow
Taffeta

HEAVY SUMMER BLOOMERS (All roses should produce summer bloom if well watered.)

Charlotte Armstrong
Eclipse
Sierra Glow
Saturnia
Neige Parfum

Pedrálbes
Peace
Texas Centennial
Etoile de Hollande
Girona
Korovo

FORTY-NINER

*"A Rose of vivid coloring with petals
yellow outside and red inside"*

ᨠ 6 ᨠ

PLANTING INSTRUCTIONS

How To Make a Bed

MUCH OF YOUR LUCK depends on the way you prepare your bed. Unless you have a teen age son, Mrs. Beginner, to be bribed away from football, or a husband willing to be lured from golf into a little digging, you had better cast your eye among your relatives to find who is still blessed with a Yard Man. If you can hire Cousin Lina Belle's Sim for a day now and then, it will brighten the domestic atmosphere of your own household.

With the assistance of Sim, shall we say, get your bed ready *at least* a month before planting time, leaving it slightly above the surrounding level. After it has settled, it will be slightly below the surrounding level.

There are as many methods of making a bed as of making a cake. Here is a recipe that has been tested.

Have Sim dig down two feet. Although some authorities are content with one and a half feet, and some lax mortals with twelve inches, since your bed is small, don't you think you might as well go the whole depth and dig two feet? If you are a housekeeper who does a bang-up job of fall cleaning because you can sail by on your efforts for a long time to come, you will not weaken at thought of two feet.

But whatever depth you choose, save your good topsoil, if any. Discard the mean subsoil. In the event your roses are to be planted near trees, do a thorough job of removing roots. The trees won't know the difference, but the roses will!

Proper drainage is absolutely essential. Sandy soil offers no trouble in this line, but it has always been routine to suggest a 5-10-inch bottom layer of rocks or cinders for clay soil. Experiments at the Agricultural Station of Virginia Polytechnic Institute showed that nothing is gained by using rocks without an outlet in the bottom of the trench. A minor engineering problem looms up here! The North Carolina Agricultural Extension Service further records that although tile drainage is best, a 10-inch layer of cobblestones or coarse gravel, laid in the bottom of the bed and in a ditch from the bed to a lower level, will serve the purpose.

The well-known hybridizer, the late Dr. J. H. Nicolas, objected to rocks—and do you want three guesses why? Because they are not absorbent! He advocated the use of porous clinkers, giving the reason that they absorb water, quickly drain the topsoil, and act as a reservoir during droughts. And so it goes!

Since I have had no experience with clay soil, I would advise you, if such is your inheritance, to consult with a successful rosarian in your locality. Established custom dies hard, and certainly the rocks without an outlet, or the cinders, have been doing no harm all these years. If you had counted on being a mere foot-and-a-half digger, however, you will have to add an extra five or six inches for your rock quarry or cinder stratum.

At this stage of the game plan to be Sim's shadow. Remember that you are the Keeper of the Show, who pulls the strings to put that sturdy back, those calloused palms, into motion.

Let him dump into the empty bed wheelbarrow-loads of cow manure, and sprinkle a light snow-flurry of superphosphate over the surface. Before the war I might have insisted also on sulphate of potash, may I say about one-tenth as much as of the superphosphate. Potash, however, whether muriate or sulphate, is still on the ungettable, if unforgettable, list.

Now, with or without potash, instruct Sim to throw in as much topsoil as needed and spade together thoroughly. For your roses to benefit from it, superphosphate should be well diffused through the soil; otherwise, it will remain little changed over a long period. Because Sim is allergic to reading, wisdom suggests that you notice what sack the "superphosphate" comes out of, else your bed might wind up with a coating of the plaster mix left over from that little remodeling job of last summer. Recalling the dainty columbine plants he recently trod upon, you will for the first time appreciate Sim's out-sized feet as he shovels along and tramps methodically to help settle the soil.

The rocks are, of course, your bottom, and this your second layer; but if you do not use rocks, this is your bottom layer.

A good proportion for your nine-or-ten-inch top layer where the roots are to go is: one-fourth clay, one-fourth humus (decayed oak leaves, alfalfa or kudzu meal, moats, or what-have-you) and one-half garden soil, the idea being that it is safer for the roots not to come in direct contact with manure, which might be too fresh. If you have clay loam already, incorporate plenty of organic material, and proceed.

How to Plant a Rose Bush

Rose roots are living things. Teach Sim to treat them as such. Since you have gone to considerable pains to buy bushes budded on understock best suited to your climate,* take care of those roots. Hear what Archibald Rutledge has to say:

"Whenever it is necessary for me to handle stock with bare roots, I have a tub full of clay water of the consistency of buttermilk. The roots are kept in this; then, when a plant is lifted out, the roots never really get exposed to the air.

* See page 56.

It seems a principle of Nature that air, especially wind, is fatal to roots. Healthy bushes with bare roots, even if kept in the sun and air for but a few minutes, may be practically dead when planted. Roots belong underground."

Never plant a dried-out rose bush. If your order has been delayed in transit, bury the plants, tops and all, for a few days until the canes have plumped out. Expertly packed bushes will reach you in prime condition after crossing the United States, the roots remaining moist in the package for several days longer, if circumstances do not permit immediate planting. In case there is to be considerable delay, heel the bushes in. If you have received poorly packed plants, almost dead upon arrival, change your nurseryman.

When the great moment arrives, remove the wrapping from the roots, which you will promptly put, as recommended, in a bucket full of clay water. Have Sim dig where you want the bush to go, laying aside the topsoil. In the hole next show Sim how to make a cone-shaped *mound* of soil upon which to place the crown of the roots, spreading them to cover as much surface as possible. Step by step, supervise as he fills in with topsoil, *treads firm* with both feet, and waters twice to close airpockets, even though the ground is already damp. Compliment Sim on the good job he's doing, telling him that loose planting is a common cause of failure. After the water settles, have him fill in with more soil, but not tread again. Take note that a correctly planted bush in the South should have the little "knob" at ground level or slightly above; on tree roses this knob should be barely covered.

Do not think your task finished until you have *mounded* a second time. This temporary mound of a few inches of soil will prevent the canes from drying out, and will protect them against a sudden freeze. You should remove it after growth starts and after danger of heavy frosts is past.

For a rose bush to be used as a shrub or a specimen, dig the hole two feet deep and two feet in diameter.

You have heard it said, "Do not put new wine in old

skins." Neither plant a new rose bush in an old hole, where another rose bush has died. In a small garden you will not be able to practice rotation of crops, but you can at least rotate the soil. Play the little game called, "Robbing Peter and Paying Paul." Transfer the rich earth which surrounded the defunct rose bush to the camellia bed, and bring some new, clean dirt back to your new rose bush.

When to Plant a Rose Bush

What is the best month for you to plant your roses? January is the accepted date in the vicinity of New Orleans, Louisiana, and Augusta, Georgia, February in Greenville, South Carolina, and March in the coldest portions of the South. Below the Mason and Dixon Line I can find but few advocates of planting before December. Although a rose bush may be completely dormant, when set out earlier it is apt to make untimely growth, which will be nipped in a heavy freeze.

Follow-up Treatment in the Spring

After "unmounding," give a top dressing of cow manure. (Some day I mean to write a poem on the power of manure!) On newly set plants avoid commercial fertilizer the first season. Keep your spade sharpened, and twice a year cut off and remove any tree or shrubbery roots that come foraging.

Also cut out completely any suckers sprouting from below the bud union and identified by entirely different foliage. Don't listen to the old wives' tale that only suckers have seven leaflets. Any self-respecting Hybrid Tea will oftentimes develop leaves composed of seven leaflets. If in doubt, delay. It is drastic to confuse suckers with the reddish ground canes developing from around the bud union, for they are the best wood on a rose bush.

Many Hybrid Teas, you will note, have a cluster of three

or more buds to a stem; these you will have to disbud for finest bloom. Give the matter your microscopic attention, and as soon as you can handle the buds (when they are the size of a tiny pea or even smaller), catch hold of the outer ones with your thumb and forefinger, pull out and down, snapping them off clean. The center bud will then be able to develop its maximum beauty.

On varieties that produce inferior flowers in hot weather, pinch off all buds for six weeks in midsummer. Play up to magnificent October bloom.

Polyanthas bloom in sprays, and are not disbudded.

ᵉᵍ᎓ 7 ᒣᵉᵍᵎ

DO'S AND DON'T'S OF PRUNING

How to Prune

HYBRID TEAS

Consider pruning a garden event worthy of your time and personal attention. There's no use asking the Yard Man, "Sim, do you know how to prune roses?"—you will receive the inevitable answer, "Yes, ma'am, I always does Miss Lina Belle's roses. I'm a right neat pruner."

As a warning there will come to your mind a picture of Cousin Lina Belle's rose bed, looking as though a whirling dervish with scimitar in hand had decapitated every bush, meting out the same punishment to the tall and the short, the strong and the weak. A clutter of twiggy growth remains, and old foliage to carry over last year's blackspot to next spring's tender leaves.

Not to hurt Sim's feelings and to train him in the way he should go, you might permit him to help. But with your program well in mind, have it definitely understood that you belong in the ranks of moderate pruners. The old dictum, "When in doubt, prune hard," originated in the cold North, where there is little alternative after winter damage. Also remember that the plan is to keep the center of the bush open for the passage of light and air, in order to check disease.

You will have already invested in a good pair of pruning shears of the scissors type with very sharp blades. With these in hand, study each plant as a separate problem. Stoop down and select the newer canes of lighter green, which you will play up to for next year's growth. Old wood which has many wounds or which would obstruct the new canes will head your Black List. Remove it with a clean cut, flush with the bud union, but keep enough old wood to retain the shape of the bush.

Leave no stubs to die back and infect sound wood. Search for the "eyes" (little pimples) on the outside of the canes which you have decided to keep. Locate an eye which would mark about one-half of last year's growth, and make a slanting cut one-fourth inch above it. The eye will be on the high side of the cut. If in doubt, prune high. You may always come back and cut above a lower eye, but after the bush is pruned, how can you even by taking thought add a cubit to its stature? Clip out all twigs. Gather up to burn all trimmings and old leaves, whether on the bush or on the ground.

POLYANTHAS, FLORIBUNDAS, AND TEAS

You need give these only the thinning treatment.

STANDARDS

You should prune standards like bush roses, with the intention of developing a symmetrical head of moderate size.

CLIMBERS

If you have sufficient space, you may leave your exuberant climbers unshorn, merely removing in the course of time branches which have outlived their usefulness. Later you may cut out altogether any blind shoots when they obscure the bloom.

Hybrid Teas, climbers as well as bushes, are sent to you already pruned. Do not shorten the long canes on the climbers or they might revert to the bush type. Each year at pruning time remove as much as feasible of the oldest

Plant Pat. No. 455

CHARLOTTE ARMSTRONG
"Cross between Soeur Therese and Crimson Glory.
No wonder it's a grand Rose!"

wood on your established climbing Hybrid Teas and tie the new canes in place. Then, as soon as the flowers are spent, shorten the blooming stems about six inches, but not the canes.

When to Prune

Do not prune your bushes back too early. The proper time is the end of the dormant period, following the last deep dip of the mercury. As to exactly when that will be, Sim's guess is as good as yours, or probably better. Although the Weather Bureau lists March 14 as the average date for the last killing frost in spring at Augusta, Georgia, I vary the actual pruning time according to the severity of the season. Usually it is the last week in February, when the leaf buds are beginning to swell, but before growth has started. Mid-March is right for Greenville, South Carolina.

The budding-out which occurs during a warm spell in January is inevitably caught in a February freeze. Since growth starts at the tip ends, the blasted eyes on the top twigs, which you will remove anyway at pruning time, will have served to deter the opening of the lower eyes. There is the opposite danger of waiting too late to prune, however; for after the sap has risen, bleeding to such an extent that tree paint will not hold may cause considerable damage.

After Pruning

SPRAYING WITH BORDEAUX—an after-pruning requisite

Buy only a small quantity of prepared Bordeaux Mixture at a time, as it deteriorates when left in the package from one year to the next; however, it is health insurance for many other plants in the garden. Mix dormant strength Bordeaux (10 tablespoonfuls to the gallon of water) and strain through a fine wire sieve or piece of cheesecloth into the sprayer, if yours is of the "golf bag," compressed-air variety. Despite the fact that there may not be any scientific authority for this advice, wet the ground as well as the bushes. When you reach the climbers and find lice on the tiny leaves, add a teaspoon-and-a-half of Black Leaf 40 to the gallon of spray. After you have finished, remind Sim to rinse out the sprayer and hang it up to drain. Inspect the nozzle and strainer to see that he keeps them clean.

If the job of spraying falls to your lot, you might investigate one of these new trombone models, with bent tip to reach the underside of leaves, and a weighted hose to drop down into your bucket of spray. I call it the Lady Gardener's Friend, because it operates easily and requires only a few pumpings of clear water to clean it.

Some folk object to the resultant blue color from the use of Bordeaux. If you think of it rather as a charm to ward off dreaded blights, in the manner of window and door-sills painted blue by old-timey darkies to keep out "ha'nts," you will not mind it. No matter if Bordeaux displeases you, do not be led into the folly of substituting lime sulphur, as advocated by some specialists. Even if you heroically endure its noisome odor, convinced that it must be greatly benefiting the roses, it will stain your white fence a gruesome brown that no amount of soap, sweat, and tears will completely remove.

PAINTING CUTS

There are two schools of thought on painting cuts—the Do and the Don't. If you side with the "Do's," within the week go back and seal all cuts with an asphalt tree paint, applying it handily with a tongue depressor. In case you turn this chore over to Sim, caution him not to get grit on the depressor and carry germs to the cut ends.

If, however, you prefer the easier course, you may line up with the Sharp Shears Crowd, who take care not to crush the stems and philosophically cut out any borers that chance along afterwards.

Summer Pruning

Avoid so-called summer pruning. This does not mean that you may not eliminate all dead and yellowed wood, as well as undesirable center and twiggy growth. Cutting blooms with long stems is in itself a form of pruning, and if you do it intelligently, there will be little need for heavy summer pruning.

8

SPRAYING AND DUSTING

The Problems

SPRAYING AND DUSTING are like giving cod liver oil and diphtheria punctures to babies. The bother is far outweighed by the joy that science has discovered these things to keep our darlings healthy. A bit of understanding will undoubtedly minimize the task. Fungicides combat diseases, but because there are also bugs, insecticides are called for, too. Some of these materials come in both spray and dust form, but there are times when spraying is more effective. Although a workable sprayer is an absolute necessity in any garden, a good dust gun can greatly lighten your labors, Milady Gardener. Probably the reason some people are averse to dusting is the inadequate type of equipment usually offered for sale. Take home one of those flimsy tin can models, resembling the pea shooter made by your Fourth Grade son, have the dust shoot out of the wrong end into your face, and you will become a ready convert to spraying.

Some commercial dusts are put up in cardboard guns, which, however, are never very satisfactory. For only a few plants the small bellows and pint jar duster will serve nicely, if you attach longer handles. Formerly there was an excellent bellows model of German origin, but it has not been available since the war. My favorite for an average planting is the sturdy two-quart plunger type, with handle for greater convenience and long extension with deflector to reach the vulnerable underside of leaves. The extension is important, the new dusts being somewhat less than a throat and eye tonic, and the color of Fermate, a principal ingredient, being black. What's the use of breathing more of this or any other chemical than you have to? And who wants to wear a mask, so politely suggested by the manufacturer? He failed to tell you, however, that a dash or two of Charles of the Ritz deodorant is helpful in ridding your arms and hands of Fermate's faint, clinging aroma.

Dusting is really not a bad job, if you go about it in the right way. Nor is it hard to do a good job, if you bide your time until the air is still. Remember, it required technique even to administer little Susie's cod liver oil!

Do not deposit blobs in some places, entirely skipping others. Applied to dry foliage, a dust is barely discernible. Learn to work from the base of a plant, letting a cloud of dust blow upwards, to settle down in a fine film on the tops of the leaves. If necessary, direct a light whiff from above. It is not only expensive to use a heavy coat, with the mounting cost of materials, but injurious to the plants as well.

For maximum efficiency, your health program must begin early and extend late. To start off on the right foot for spring, spray at pruning time with Bordeaux, and when the roses have signed off for the winter, give them a final clean-up spray of Bordeaux.

In the interim: As soon as the new leaves appear, begin a weekly dusting routine, which will become almost second nature, akin to perpetual motion. Spring is the critical period. Do not allow the lush foliage to fool you into thinking that your plants will possess a charmed immunity. They won't!

You may use one of the complete commercial dusts,* which are a combination fungicide-insecticide, or alternate its use with a fungicide to take care of the two major maladies, mildew and blackspot. Mildew is a "skin" disease,

* See page 43.

which can with difficulty be dried up or cured; it can more easily be prevented. Blackspot, which does an inside job, must be prevented; it cannot be cured. To control them both, combine nine parts of 325 mesh dusting sulphur and, further to control blackspot but not mildew, one part of Fermate. If you prefer, you may purchase duPont Rose Dust, which is the same formula, but it is much cheaper to mix your own. While you count, have Sim measure the ingredients into a can, add a few round stones, fasten the lid, and roll for thorough mixing.

Spring is the strategic time not only to circumvent diseases but to take all-out action against unwelcome visitors. Despite any preventive treatment, aphids have a sudden way of holding Protracted Meeting on all of the new growth, and they do not bring along their lunches but picnic on the tender buds. Since this is one of those occasions when the force of a fine spray is more effective than a dust, do not promise yourself, "I will have Sim get rid of these vandals the first thing next week." Instead, remember that worthy's homespun expression, "When the barn has kotch afire, you cain't set down and wait on rain"—but go after them, yourself, with a nicotine spray ($1\frac{1}{2}$ teaspoonfuls of Black Leaf 40 and either a teaspoonful of Ivory flakes or a half teaspoonful of Dreft to the gallon of water). To catch them all, it may be necessary to spray two or three days in succession, but the following day, dust again. Your "complete" sulphur or summertime copper-rotenone dust will probably hold aphids in check until another onslaught in the fall.

The perfect set-up for a leprous attack of mildew seems to be high humidity, the moderate temperature of spring and fall, and succulent growth produced by high nitrogen and low potash. This, again, is an instance when a spray is required. Several applications may be needed before this oily growth can be eradicated, the dosage being two tablespoonfuls of wettable sulphur and a half teaspoonful of Dreft to the gallon of water. Although this white plague is not so prevalent in the South as blackspot, it pays to follow a program of prevention.

Blackspot, on the other hand, is like the poor that we have with us always. And may I repeat that blackspot cannot be cured? Indeed, leaflets with but a single spot are doomed; they have received the kiss of death and will spread contagion through the garden. Give them short shrift; pluck them off. Cremation should be their lot.

Was blackspot your personal problem when the rains came in the spring, inspiring climbing Mrs. Sam McGredy to stupendous growth, but demoralizing your spraying schedule? Before the main blooming season was barely over, did this lovely lady become the mere skeleton of her former self, with yellowed leaves sadly dangling, or blown in drifts down at her feet? Blackspot may be incurable, but do not place Mrs. Sam, herself, upon the funeral pyre. Try a bit of pruning that you probably skipped over in the winter, pick off steadily all affected leaves, spray or dust with sulphur and Fermate, fertilize lightly, water heavily, and put Mrs. Sam back on the road to health. You will miss some of her secondary bloom, but give her reasonable attention, and she will respond in the fall with her usual hearty greeting.

Summer poses a problem, because sulphur scorches foliage when the thermometer rises in the neighborhood of ninety degrees. In border-line weather, if you are fearful that sulphur might burn your Crimson Glories, which seem particularly susceptible, apply it toward evening so that there will be a gradual suffusion of the fumes with the early morning sun. Injury occurs when the hot sun drives off the fumes too rapidly. The complete commercial dusts, compounded for year-round use in cooler climates, have a sulphur content of only 15-40 per cent and may be used later in the spring than straight dusting sulphur.

The American Rose Society recommends using talc as a carrier for Fermate in hot weather. You will not find this a very practicable plan, for although talc and pyrophyllite are mined in the South, they are not offered for sale in any retail stores.

During our long, hot, and humid summers, possibly the easiest, safest, and most economical procedure is to change over to a copper dust, which several manufacturers mix conveniently with rotenone. For good measure, give an occasional "treatment" with duPont Garden Dust, and even such public enemies as Midge and Thrips should be held in check. Of course, when cool weather returns in the fall, you may switch back to your sulphur formula.

In conclusion, a few words of advice: no matter if it sounds backwards, dust before rains. Your dust will not be completely washed away, but redistributed on the foliage. After a rain, give another light coating. Make your schedule fairly flexible. You may be able to relax your efforts somewhat in hot, dry spells, but you want to be on the alert in wet weather, or during periods of heavy morning dews. It seems superfluous to add that if you are ready to cut roses, do so before, not after, applications.

Pandora's Box: Contents

(Here's hoping that the lid will be kept tight so that these evil insects may not escape into your garden! A hand lens will help you keep on the lookout, for some of these pests are almost invisible.)

APHIDS—tiny (usually green) sucking lice on the new growth and underside of leaves, deforming buds and new foliage.

Rx: Black Leaf 40, with Dreft or soapflakes to act as spreader and to help liberate the nicotine.
Rotenone (which gives a slow kill, its residue effective for nearly a week). D.D.T. not effective.

ROSE SLUGS (Borers)—caterpillar-like larva stage of the sawfly. Puncture pruned ends of stems.

Rx: Asphalt tree paint as a preventative.

Also puncture young growth below a flower bud, causing wilting. Eat holes in leaves, which turn brown, as if with "rust."

Rx: Arsenate of lead (incompatible with soap). D.D.T.

LEAFHOPPERS—slender, differently colored jumpers, feeding on underside of leaves, which turn grayish, stippled, sometimes curling.

Rx: D.D.T. Black Leaf 40 with Dreft or soapflakes. Copper and rotenone.

THRIPS—minute, slender insects, attacking flower buds and rasping edges of petals, which sometimes turn brown and fail to open. Foliage, silver-specked. Thrips use weeds as hide-outs.

Rx: D.D.T.

MIDGE—a late summer pest. Turns smallest buds black and dry, blackens eyes in leaf axils. Distorts older buds and kills new shoots. White maggots feed at base of flower buds. Growth, twiggy; stems, short. Absence of summer and fall bloom.

Rx: D.D.T. on bush and ground.

RED SPIDER—hot weather, orange-colored mites, spinning cobwebs from leaf to leaf and on underside of leaves, which yellow and fall.

Rx: Strong rotenone spray with Dreft or soapflakes. Make three applications within 2 weeks. D.D.T. not effective; in fact, may promote Red Spider.

MEALY BUGS—kin to scale. Flat, oval, white bugs, radiating projections. Secrete white fluid like dried soapsuds on canes and underside of leaves. Infest shrubbery, transferring to roses, especially heavy climbers in shade.

Rx: for shrubbery. Spray thoroughly with Florida Volck and Black Leaf 40. Volck incompatible with sulphur. Avoid midday heat or temperature above 85°.

Rx: for roses. Since Mealy Bugs are prevalent during hot weather in May, when the rose bushes have probably been sulphur dusted within the month, it is safer to spray with Black Leaf 40 (2 teaspoonfuls to the gallon of water, plus a half teaspoonful of Dreft.)

SCALE—incrustation of white scales; attacks neglected climbers.

Rx: When young are crawling, spray with Volck and Black Leaf 40. Cut out heavily coated canes at base and burn.

NEMATODE—a lowly worm, causing small knots on roots, and matting rootlets. Stunts growth.

Rx: D.D. (fumigant) to soil.

The A. B. C.'s

1. Paste the card of instructions that comes on your sprayer in your Garden Notebook for ready reference.

2. When the disc holes wear too large to make a fine spray, order new discs for your compressed-air sprayer.

3. Dusting Instructions—Plunger Model: Fill the hopper only ¾ full. Use quick strokes rather than slow, easy ones. When you wish to reverse the direction of the dust, turn the deflector over. You can't use the duster upside-down; the handle is on the top side. Label and put away in a safe place the envelope of powdered graphite for lubricating the plunger.

4. Be sure your rose bushes are not suffering for water when you dust or spray.

5. Since no spray is kind to white paint, apply at an angle to spare your fence or garage as much as possible.

6. The verb "spray" is not spelled s-p-r-i-n-k-l-e. Nor is it spelled d-r-e-n-c-h. Too much spray is wasteful and discolors foliage. Tap the foliage lightly with a stick to empty puddles which may collect.

7. Spray must be used immediately after mixing. Dust

Plant Pat. No. 337

MME. HENRI GUILLOT
*"A newcomer among the climbers, whose large buds open
to camellia-like flowers of rich raspberry hue"*

may remain handily in the gun for a quick pick-up or patching job.

8. Dusts that are colored green stain blooms.

9. It is more economical to buy spraying and dusting materials in the larger-sized package, containing 3 or 4 pounds.

10. Map out your year's spraying and dusting program in advance, and then give it a fair trial. A little headwork will save your pocketbook.

Check-up on Advertised Products, for Your Convenience

JACKSON & PERKINS DUST, ORTHO-DUST, PROTEXALL DUST, TRIO-GEN DUST, etc.

representing the most popular Rose Dust formula—sulphur from 20-40 per cent; Fermate; D.D.T.; rotenone; and other cubé resins to act as a miticide against a possible Red Spider infestation from use of D.D.T.

DUPONT FLORAL DUST

following the above formula, with the substitution of the new duPont chemical, methoxychlor (trade name Marlate 50) for D.D.T. (This analogue or chemical cousin is less toxic to warm-blooded animals than D.D.T., and has about the same killing potential for insects.) May be used as dust or spray, but spray is disfiguring to open blooms.

ENDOPEST

(product of Swift & Co.) containing 15 per cent sulphur, Zerlate (the zinc and white counterpart of Fermate, but not so extensively tested as Fermate), phenothyazine, rotenone, and other cubé resins.

DUPONT ROSE DUST

a fungicide, containing sulphur and Fermate.

DUPONT GARDEN DUST

containing Fermate, Zerlate, D.D.T., and rotenone. An excellent garden dust or spray, but manufacturers suggest amateurs use it with discretion on roses, and only as a dust (not a spray) when there is bloom.

JACKSON & PERKINS SPRAY, PROTEXALL SPRAY

similar formula to dust.

TRIOGEN SPRAY

containing copper, Fermate, and insecticides. For the small Southern gardener, not interested in fitting a remedy to each ill, this is a safe, year-round spray offering reasonable protection.

NIAGARA C O C S COPPER DUST, WILSON'S COP-O-RITE DUST

representing a copper-rotenone combination, which may be used on dry or damp foliage. Recommended for summer.

⋘ 9 ⋙

SEASONAL CARE

Summer Care: Suggestions

IN SUMMER when our Southland is saturated with sunshine, what relief can you suggest for the roses?

Shade?

But what kind of shade? Roses planted in full shade or even in a pine thicket, ever striving for the sun, grow to gangling heights. They will find the air-conditioning pleasant enough in midsummer, but without sunlight to manufacture flowers, there will be a dearth of fall bloom.

Well, what about a compromise—planting varieties which can "take it" in the bed lying in full sun, and those preferring semi-shade in more favorable spots in the garden?

An excellent suggestion! But is that all that you can do?

Close planting—letting the tops grow together to shade the roots?

No. I wouldn't advise it, for it will reduce the number of leaves and flowers. You want well-rounded bushes, not naked canes with a topknot of foliage and bloom. Eighteen-inch spacing is a Northern specification. In the South thirty inches is the minimum, many huskies or sprawlers liking more.

Summer dormancy?

No, indeed! As a deliberate practice from conviction, or induced from lack of care—it matters not how it is arrived at—the effect is the same—bad. On the contrary, keep dead flower heads picked off, and your plants growing along, lightly fed, but well mulched, well watered, and well clothed. Since roses, like every one else, will profit from a little vacation, you may try out the Greenville, South Carolina, Six Weeks' Plan of pinching off buds in midsummer on all but your heavy bloomers. Then at the first breath of cool weather they will be ready to snap into action and give a good account of themselves in the production line.

Just a trifle sarcastic, you say, "What about a temporary lattice frame overhead? That plan works well out at the foot of the Sierra Nevada Mountains, where it sometimes gets hotter than Hades."

Since you dot your garden every summer with "chicken-coop" structures to protect your young camellias, why should you laugh at the idea of a sunshade for your roses? At the height of the camellia season do you hesitate to place over each of your new grafts an old battery jar, shrouded with a crocus sack, topped off with a brick, making one think that so many Bedouins of the desert are encamped in your Boxwood border?

Although I have toyed with the thought of a removable framework over a small bed well out of the public eye, I have never tried such a drastic solution to the summer problem. It still tempts me, but all that I urge you to do is not to forget any of the little tricks and turns. As you stroll through your garden of a summer evening, you do not wish your roses to reproach you thus: "You have left undone those things which you ought to have done; you have done those things which you ought not to have done; and there is no health in us!"

Among other things, be a mulcher. A two-inch mulch of peat moss, oak leaves, or pine needles, etc, is an absolute summer necessity. You must dig in lightly your manure mulch when first the sun beams down hot. You may then add your summer mulch or, if you prefer, broadcast seed of low-growing and shallow-rooted annuals to form a living mulch, particularly in your formal bed. Rose bushes in your border will benefit from such treatment, too, keeping the taller flowers at a proper distance to allow circulation of air. As soon as these annuals become shabby, you may pull them up, fertilize, water, and if practicable, re-sow; if not, content yourself with a neat layer of the usually-accessible pine needles. Since mulches gradually decompose, you will need to replenish yours from time to time.

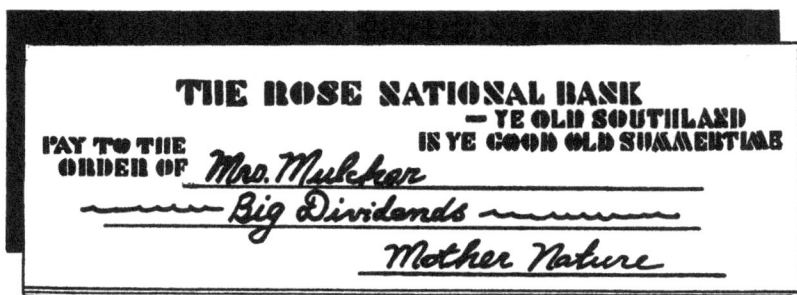

THE ROSE NATIONAL BANK
— YE OLD SOUTHLAND
IN YE GOOD OLD SUMMERTIME
PAY TO THE ORDER OF *Mrs. Mulcher*
Big Dividends
Mother Nature

Although a mulch helps to hold moisture, it goes without saying that if you spare the water, you will spoil the roses.

Carpet your yard with a lawn of as deep a pile as your water bill will permit. It will lower the temperature not only of your roses' living quarters, but also your family's summer quarters, the porch.

Get as lackadaisical as you like about your dusting program indoors—but not outdoors!

And in case you find all of this very arduous, just read the chapter on "Winter Care in Connecticut" in any good garden book!

Winter Care

Four inches of oak leaves and/or pine straw make a light, warm coverlet for your established roses in winter. The bud union is most subject to frost damage, and should receive some protection. Hilling up or mounding old plants with soil is necessary in only the coldest portions of the South.

Remove this winter cover when applying a manure mulch in earliest spring.

FROST DATA *

The average date of first killing frost in fall and of last killing frost in spring.

	FIRST IN FALL	LAST IN SPRING
Blacksburg, Va.	Oct. 11	Apr. 26
Roanoke, Va.	Oct. 22	Apr. 15
Lynchburg, Va.	Oct. 25	Apr. 4
Winston-Salem, N. C.	Oct. 25	Apr. 11
Durham, N. C.	Oct. 27	Apr. 9
Tryon, N. C.	Oct. 29	Apr. 15
Florence, Ala.	Oct. 29	Apr. 5
Chapel Hill, N. C.	Nov. 1	Apr. 5
Hattiesburg, Miss.	Nov. 1	Mar. 13
Richmond, Va.	Nov. 2	Mar. 29
Knoxville, Tenn.	Nov. 2	Mar. 30
Spartanburg, S. C.	Nov. 3	Mar. 31
Rome, Ga.	Nov. 3	Mar. 31
Athens, Ga.	Nov. 5	Apr. 2
Newport News, Va.	Nov. 6	Mar. 29
Jackson, Miss.	Nov. 8	Mar. 19
Raleigh, N. C.	Nov. 9	Mar. 23
Atlanta, Ga.	Nov. 9	Mar. 23
Memphis, Tenn.	Nov. 10	Mar. 17
Greenville, S. C.	Nov. 10	Mar. 27
Birmingham, Ala.	Nov. 11	Mar. 16
Macon, Ga.	Nov. 11	Mar. 16
Charlotte, N. C.	Nov. 11	Mar. 18
Meridian, Miss.	Nov. 11	Mar. 17
Chattanooga, Tenn.	Nov. 11	Mar. 21
Natchez, Miss.	Nov. 13	Mar. 13
Augusta, Ga.	Nov. 13	Mar. 14
Shreveport, La.	Nov. 15	Mar. 8
Vicksburg, Miss.	Nov. 15	Mar. 8
Columbus, Ga.	Nov. 16	Mar. 12
Columbia, S. C.	Nov. 18	Mar. 15
Montgomery, Ala.	Nov. 19	Mar. 3
Baton Rouge, La.	Nov. 20	Feb. 24
Thomasville, Ga.	Nov. 20	Mar. 6
Savannah, Ga.	Nov. 28	Feb. 28
Biloxi, Miss.	Nov. 29	Feb. 26
Charleston, S. C.	Dec. 5	Feb. 23
New Orleans, La.	Dec. 9	Feb. 20

* Source: *Climate and Man.* U. S. Department of Agriculture, 1941.

Plant Pat. No. 105

CRIMSON GLORY
"One of the world's great Roses"

10

WATERING

BECAUSE LEAVES are the roses' breathing apparatus
and food manufactory, the object of the game you are
playing is to keep as many of them as possible growing in
healthy condition on your rose bushes. Blackspot, which
breeds in dampness, causes defoliation; therefore your
method of watering is vitally important. Remove the nozzle
from the hose and thoroughly soak the ground, trying not
to spatter the foliage and wash off your floral dust. During
a prolonged drought, for appearance's sake, you may like
to rinse off the foliage, but as soon as it is dry, give it a
fresh "coat of armor."

You afternoon waterers should remember this equation:
Rose foliage $+$ 6 hrs. dampness $-$ a fungicide $=$ blackspot.

The answer to this problem is:

Water the rest of your garden, if it is more convenient, in
the afternoon, but if possible save your roses for morning,
when their foliage will dry promptly. While the weather
stays hot, you will be repaid for early rising by finding
both the garden and the water pressure at their best. Be
lazy enough to think it smart, however, to use a canvas soil
soaker and the new featherweight plastic hose, as well as a
deep mulch to hold the moisture and make cultivation un-
necessary. Provided you are generous enough with the
water, dependables like Peace and Charlotte Armstrong

will reward you with bloom all summer, and Mme. Henri Guillot with fall flowers that are unrivaled.

Truly, if roses were vocal, the summer lament in many a Southern garden would be:

Res-cue the per-ish-ing Care for the dy-ing

∽ 11 ⧉

CUTTING ROSES

CUTTING ROSES MAKES a delightful topic. We are told that late afternoon is the best time, because sugar, which the leaves manufacture when the sun shines, adds to the keeping quality of the cut flower. Early morning is the next best time. Don't rush out with the scissors in hand and a Delilah gleam in your eye, to shear the newly set bushes of all their bloom and strength; let them build up into robust plants. Nor should you rob even an established plant of all its growth. Particularly in the spring, try to cut your longest stems from first one bush and then another. Mrs. Flower Arranger, if you are planning to use those full-blown Crimson Glories for your "focal point," why take more stem than you actually need? In late summer and fall it will be quite safe to indulge your weakness for very long stems. Climbing Hybrid Teas, I hasten to add, are the cutter's delight; in their case, you may cut your roses and keep your bushes, too! Standards, which require a sort of seasonal pruning to remain shapely, often permit the taking of handsome stems.

You will find that a small, light-weight pair of pruning shears, with a slide button for opening and locking, is ideal for cutting roses. Incidentally, the psychological effect of the shears is good, for they remind you to take care of your bushes. Do not snip blooms haphazardly, leaving an inch or two of stem to develop canker, but always cut one-fourth inch above a leaf. In the axil of that leaf is an eye, which will produce a new stem and flowers. This rule applies also to removing dead flower heads.

If you own a wide-mouthed battery jar, left over from grafting camellias, station it near a spigot in your garden. It will be easy for you then, as soon as you cut your roses, to plunge them in water up to their necks. When you bring the roses indoors, remove the lower leaves and thorns. (Some people recommend splitting the ends of the stems a half-inch, but this makes for poor anchorage with a needle holder.) Then pinch off carefully any damaged petals, and wash all spray off the foliage with cotton kept at hand for the purpose, or a piece of nylon stocking.

My further advice is to add ice cubes to the water, but take no stock in chemicals to prolong the life of the blossoms. Roses from the florist's may need such help, but yours won't! After a "conditioning" period in your cool basement, they will be equipped for their career above stairs. It will probably amuse you that the newest wrinkle is to keep the basement light on, if holding red roses for any length of time, to prevent their color from "bluing."

Let your roses become your ambassadors of good will—but when sending them to your friends, be sure that they look well-groomed.

⚜ 12 ⚜

FACTS FOR FILING

ORGANIC FERTILIZERS are derived from animal products; inorganic, from minerals.

Organic Fertilizers

Good rose soil must contain adequate amounts of organic matter (humus), which needs to be replaced frequently. The following forms are recommended:

COW MANURE—Also a fertilizer, containing a moderate quantity of nitrogen and potash, with some phosphoric acid. Contributes beneficent bacteria. Slightly alkaline reaction.

COMPOST—Every thrifty gardener keeps a compost pile. Generally no fertilizing value.

PEAT MOSS—Also the best known mulch. No fertilizing value. Slightly acid reaction.

MOATS (cotton waste)—If allowed to go through a heat, decompose into black humus. Before decomposition, will burn plants and produce myriads of weeds. No fertilizing value.

Inorganic Fertilizers

NITROGEN—Stimulates soft, lush growth. An excess of nitrogen (1) injures feeder roots; (2) makes foliage subject to blackspot and mildew; (3) makes cut roses wilt.

PHOSPHORIC ACID—Makes sturdy root and plant growth; adds to quantity and size of blooms; adds to keeping quality of cut and uncut blooms. Low phosphorus means poor flowers.

POTASH—Makes harder, more resistant growth, counteracting the soft growth from nitrogen: intensifies color of blooms; adds to keeping quality of cut and uncut blooms.

Other Favorite Fertilizers,
Both Organic and Inorganic

COTTON SEED MEAL (organic)—Contains 7 per cent nitrogen, 3 per cent phosphoric acid, 2 per cent potash. Slightly acid reaction.

ALFALFA LEAF MEAL and KUDZU MEAL (organic)—Contain 3 per cent nitrogen, 0.7 per cent phosphoric acid, 2 per cent potash, 2 per cent lime. Very slightly alkaline reaction. High humus content. Excellent for bed making.

SUPERPHOSPHATE (inorganic)—Contains 20 per cent phosphoric acid. pH 2 or 3,* but does not give acid reaction. Cheaper and more readily available than Bone Meal. Give to climbers, especially when buds are forming.

BONE MEAL (organic)—Contains 20 per cent phosphoric acid, 2-3 per cent nitrogen. Slow acting. pH 10.2 may prove misleading. Raw Bone Meal, when first applied to the soil, is slightly acid forming. Over a long period of time,

---

* pH is a symbol for the hydrogen-ion concentration of the soil, the degree of acidity or alkalinity.

soil acidity seems to be reduced slightly, but the amount is probably insignificant.

MURIATE OF POTASH (inorganic)—Contains 50 per cent potash. More readily available than Sulphate of Potash.

SULPHATE OF POTASH (inorganic)—Contains 49-51 per cent potash.

HARDWOOD ASHES (organic)—Contain 1 per cent phosphoric acid, 6 per cent potash. The word potassium, or potash, means "pot ashes." Alkaline reaction. Treasure them for your roses. But a word of caution: too much actually can be used!

Not a Fertilizer

LIME—Though not a fertilizer should always be in soil in normal supply. Form: ground limestone recommended. Helps both heavy and light soils, favoring growth of bacteria. Gives soil a better tilth. Alkaline reaction. Dosage: approximately 2 tablespoonfuls to a rose bush. Lime hastens decomposition in the compost pile.

More Facts about Fertilizer

The numerals of a "complete" fertilizer indicate ingredients in the following order: per cent of Nitrogen (N); per cent of Phosphoric Acid (P_2O_5); per cent of Potash (K_2O). Or they may indicate pounds of these elements per 100 pounds of fertilizer. For example:

1. Vigoro Formula: 4-12-4

2. Reliance Formula: 6-8-8, an excellent Azalea-Camellia special. In order to maintain proper acidity for these plants, contains small amount of aluminum sulphate, which is not recommended for roses.

3. Charles Mallerin's Personal Formula: 4-10-14. When planting beans in a rose bed, M. Mallerin fertilized it

heavily with potash for the beans. He was amazed to discover that although his other roses, receiving the same fungicidal protection as these, developed their accustomed blackspot, these were immune. Tests at Virginia Polytechnic Institute Experiment Station did not substantiate this experience, but proved the value of a fertilizer low in nitrogen, very high in phosphates, and high, if not extremely high, in potash.

Too much chemical fertilizer is almost as bad as too little.

Fertilizer burns foliage; apply carefully. Do not leave it lying on the ground for the wind to blow about. Scratch it in and water copiously. Materials can enter roots only in solution.

The traditional date for last fall fertilizing is one month before killing frost is expected. Cautious gardeners limit their final application to superphosphate and some form of potash for fine fall bloom.

Understocks

The custom of growing Hybrid Teas on their own roots is now almost extinct, practically all nurserymen budding them on wild understock. A rose is no better than its root system. It is everywhere agreed that further understock experimentation is desirable. It is known, for instance, that certain bud-understock combinations are definitely incompatible.

For you average-buyer is appended this thumb-nail sketch of recommended understocks:

MULTIFLORA JAPONICA—Best for most sections of the U.S.A. Used by all Northern nurseries. Stands low winter temperatures.

RAGGED ROBIN—Stands hot summers. A steady grower. Apt to be longer-lived than Multiflora. Suckers very little. Resistant to Nematode (important in sandy soil). Sensitive to poor drainage.

ODORATA—Stands hot summers. A steady grower. Transplants easily in nearly all soils and climates. Stands droughts as well as excess of moisture. The prevailing understock of the Italian Riviera, where its strong roots grow deeply in the arid soil and endure the long summer heat. Used extensively on the Gulf Coast and in Florida. Ragged Robin and Odorata, favorites with California nurseries, are particularly suited to the South. Hybrid Teas on these understocks, planted in late winter, quickly spring into growth and bloom.

DR. HUEY—A new variety, largely replacing Ragged Robin in Southern California. Used successfully with weak-growing Hybrid Teas.

I have used all of the above understocks with success, provided the plants were good. A poor plant, no matter what the understock, will fail.

Much Ado about pH

What is the proper pH for roses? You will discover a diversity of ideas. Our friend Dr. Nicolas, from his extensive experience in Europe and America, was convinced that a neutral soil or slightly alkaline is best; that colors are more brilliant and lasting, and foliage less subject to disease, when roses are growing in a deeply trenched, well aerated soil of a pH between 7 and 8. The soil samples which he collected from all of the leading European rose nurseries bore out his theories; however, Charles Mallerin, who originally preferred strongly alkaline soil, now recommends neutral. We come on down the pH scale to find most American authorities favoring slightly acid soil. By way of illustration: When roses would no longer grow in New Orleans, acid amendments plus organic matter rendered fertile the highly alkaline soil, which then produced beautiful bloom.

As pH is measured, each unit below neutral 7 indicates

ten times as much acidity as the preceding one, and each unit above 7 ten times as much alkalinity. Because the subject appears simple, enthusiasts without a knowledge of chemistry or soil science have rushed in with home testing sets and have begun analyzing and doctoring their own soils. Harry Daunoy, soil expert, believes, however, that the excessive use of acidifying amendments may bring about a toxic condition worse than the one it seeks to correct. It is important for you to know, moreover, that pH varies at almost every inch of the depth of the soil (it may be low at the surface and high at root level). Also, two differently textured soils of identical pH will require a different amount of lime to bring their alkalinity up a unit.

The correct pH for your roses probably cannot be summed up arbitrarily in numeral and decimal, but will depend upon your climate, as well as upon the quality of your soil. As far as I am personally concerned, I will place my bets on slightly acid soil. Last spring, when climbing Mme. Henri Guillot put on a super-colossal display, I decided to end this pH controversy, at least for local conditions, and promptly sent off a soil sample to be tested. Report: 6.3. At the same time, a neighbor's bed of The Doctor was so magnificent that I begged a soil sample. Report: 5.9!

If you are a beginner living in a locality neither excessively alkaline nor excessively acid, you may well leave this heady subject to the experts and to the gardenia growers. You will find comfort in the thought that sufficient organic matter incorporated in the soil not only acts like a sponge to hold air and water, but tends to resist any fluctuation in pH. If, however, your ambition is to become a Master Gardener, or if you run into trouble, you will certainly want to take advantage of your state's free soil analysis service.

To secure a representative sample, dig down a trowel's depth in several places in your rose bed and collect about a cup and a half of soil. A small box, like an ice-cream container, is a good receptacle to mail it in, accompanying it with a letter of explanation. Your report will show not only the pH, but the per cent of nitrogen, phosphoric acid, potash, calcium, magnesium, and organic matter in your soil—with recommendations for its improvement.

✺ 13 ✺

MODERN ROSES

Beware of Bargains!

TELL THE TRUTH. Don't you mean to open the eyes of the neighbors with top-flight bloom? Mrs. Rosarian, don't you intend to win the blue ribbon at the Garden Club? And Mr. Rosarian, don't you expect to take a choice specimen to the office with the same modest pride with which you showed off your first-born? If so, pass up those paraffined jobs at the Five-and-Ten; they aren't cheap at any price. Bargains offered by mail-order houses may even mean plants worn out in the cut-flower trade. Definitely you do not want a pindling plant, but there is no virtue in extra-sized or "super" bushes. Remember, too, that some varieties, like Snowbird and Crimson Glory, are naturally small growers.

Emphatically you desire a good root system. Although you may prefer to find out, yourself, the comparative merits of Ragged Robin, Odorata, and Multiflora for your own conditions, at least know what understocks you are receiving.

It is always wise to do your purchasing whether it be of iris, camellias, or roses, from a nursery which specializes in that particular plant. Don't lose sight of the fact that there are no bargains among the new roses, for a certain patented variety costs the same wherever it is sold. It is thrifty to go in with your neighbors or the members of your

Garden Club to secure a quantity discount. BUT BUY QUALITY!

Join the American Rose Society

It may not be amiss to say here that your best buy in the Rose World to-day is a membership in the American Rose Society.* You will be entitled to a list of consultants and fellow members as well as to the annual publication and the bi-monthly magazine, which are the last word in garden practices. And don't think that they don't change! Growing roses is a living art, not a dead or a static one. The experiments of such famous plant pathologists as Cornell's Dr. L. M. Massey will mean healthier roses for you. He constantly reports on the newest chemicals that have been tested sufficiently for garden use. Among other experts, Dr. Cynthia Westcott brings light and laughter to the melancholy subject of insects.

All gardeners agree that the hybridizers of late have introduced too many temperamental beauties. Modern roses, while infinitely more glamorous, are correspondingly less vigorous than were Grandma's favorites, whose only acquaintance with a spraying schedule was an occasional washbowl of soapy water tossed out the bedroom window onto their unsuspecting heads. Incidentally, rose bushes lived to a ripe old age in Grandma's day!

Considering the abundance of glorious bloom that I receive eight months in the year, I have no just complaints to make against the rose death rate. I am planning to set out a number of small camellias, which I shall leave behind me as a horticultural legacy when I quit this world. They will make magnificent plants for my grandchildren. But I grow roses for myself.

---

* Write the Secretary, Box 687, Harrisburg, Pa. He can give you information also on the Georgia Rose Society, Tennessee Rose Society, and affiliated Rose Societies in the following Southern cities: Portsmouth, Va., Richmond, Va., Roanoke, Va., Norfolk, Va., Chattanooga, Tenn., Knoxville, Tenn., Memphis, Tenn., Raleigh, N. C., Durham, N. C., Jackson, Miss., New Orleans, La., and a Men's Rose Society in High Point, N. C.

Before Ordering Roses

No matter if your beginning rose garden will total but a twenty dollar order, you may acquire a two hundred dollar education from the colored catalogues to be had for the asking. Don't let the orange and copper tones of Fred Edmunds be your undoing. That "good in coastal sections" is a warning that he will not hold up under our summers. You had better scratch Fred's name off your list! Did you first decide to become a rosarian when you saw a perfect bloom of The Doctor at a flower show? Although you discover now that the plant is rated one of the poorest in commerce, are you bound and determined to grow The Doctor anyway? At least you know enough to give him partial shade and your clinical attention, and if you coerce him into living, he will become your pride and joy—but there are more fool-proof pinks.

New roses which have attained top rating at the various national testing grounds are introduced each year. Peace, for instance, won the highest score on record, but we shall be lucky if Peace's equal comes along within a decade. Old American Rose Annuals are a graveyard of forgotten names, many roses never living longer than their advertising propaganda. The recently patented are, of course, the most expensive; they are not necessarily the best.

⤌ 14 ⤍

ROSE POLL

THE BIGGEST RETURNS from growing roses are the friendships that one makes. There is something definitely clannish about rosarians. Possessed of a love of the beautiful, mellowed by constant association with Mother Nature, they form a notable fraternity.

I am deeply grateful to my twenty-eight contributors to this "Gallup" Poll. Some of them are my personal friends, who in turn suggested the names of their friends. Among those represented here are owners of large estates, officials in charge of testing plots, and small gardeners like myself, who have taken the matter of rose growing very much to heart.

Lists of favorites have always fascinated me. There is hardly a grower of roses who, after searching his soul, has not tabulated those which delight him most or serve him best. Once when my husband in his capacity of C.P.A. was examining a musty set of ancient records in a neighboring cotton mill, he found in the auditor's report a final recommendation. Having certified that the finances were in excellent condition, this man of fancy as well as figures solemnly urged the directors to plant a rose garden in front of the office door. Then followed a nostalgic list, his choice among now almost forgotten beauties; of course, "reds for the gentlemen, but also pinks and whites to please the ladies."

In this Rose Poll, the contributors were asked to submit names of ten favorites, with a word of comment, if they saw fit, allowing personal preference full sway. When more were offered, the first ten made up the official count. To me the results are astonishing not because some lovely varieties received only a few votes, but because from this great big World of Roses a few were chosen by so many people. Nor should you readers scorn a rose that rated but a vote or two. Perhaps it is too new to be well known, like Debonair; or else it is an old friend elbowed aside in commerce, like climbing Columbia, but performing faithfully in the garden. R.M.S. Queen Mary, reminiscent of the ladies in Poe's poetry, may in spite of her weak frame be cherished for her ethereal beauty, or Portadown Fragrance for delicious perfume.

Now let me confidently recommend to you our winners as a perfect beginning for your small garden. To comply with the usual conception of eleven as a Rose Bowl Team, I should like to select from the substitutes either Kaiserin Auguste Viktoria to complete the color range, or Dainty Bess to represent the singles. And although it has become the style to look down our noses at members of the Radiance family, which Dr. Nicolas thought owed 99½ per cent of its popularity to its husky body, we Southerners might take a tip from Californians and experiment with growing these indestructibles as hedges.

All Southern Team: Rose Bowl Favorites

(Number of votes, in parentheses, out of a possible 29)

ETOILE DE HOLLANDE * (22), originator: H. A. Verschuren. Dutch. This ubiquitous red is too well known to need an introduction.

CRIMSON GLORY * (18), originator: Wilhelm Kordes. German. One of the world's great roses.

* Comes in both bush and climbing form.

Plant Pat. No. 172

ECLIPSE

"This Hybrid Tea Rose will flaunt an amazing quantity
of golden blooms five or six times during the year"

ECLIPSE (14), originator: J. H. Nicolas. American. Named on a total eclipse day, it has not yet been eclipsed by any yellow.

CHARLOTTE ARMSTRONG (12), originator: W. E. Lammerts. American. Cross between Soeur Thérèse and Crimson Glory. No wonder it's a grand rose! Blood red.

PEACE (11), originator: Francis Meilland, pupil of Charles Mallerin. French. Deservedly, the most publicized rose in the world.

EDITOR MCFARLAND (10), originator: Charles Mallerin. French. Clear pink, long lasting as a cut flower, it has grown well for everybody but the famous rosarian for whom it was named.

COUNTESS VANDAL * (9), originator: M. Leenders. Dutch. A moving picture in technicolor.

PICTURE * (9), originator: McGredy. Irish. A colleen exemplifying the pink of perfection. Larger flowers with more petals in the climbing form.

MADAME COCHET-COCHET (8), originator: Charles Mallerin. French. Coppery pink.

MADAME HENRI GUILLOT * (7), originator: Charles Mallerin. French. Magnificent spring and fall bloom. The temperamental star of the team.

SUBSTITUTES

KAISERIN AUGUSTE VIKTORIA * (6), white

DAINTY BESS * (5), single, pink

RED RADIANCE * (5)

MRS. CHARLES BELL (5), shell pink

CHRISTOPHER STONE * (5), red—seedling of Etoile de Hollande

To Charles Mallerin, originator of three winners on the ALL SOUTHERN TEAM, we take off our hat! He is not merely a research worker of great distinction, but a genuine dirt gardener as well.

* Comes in both bush and climbing form.

ROSES IN VIRGINIA
A. G. Smith Jr.
Specialist, Ornamental Horticulture
Blacksburg, Virginia

The following varieties have been satisfactory at the Virginia Polytechnic Institute Experimental Plots:

1. RED RADIANCE
2. PINK RADIANCE
3. KAISERIN AUGUSTE VIKTORIA
4. EDITOR MCFARLAND
5. CHARLES K. DOUGLAS
6. CRIMSON GLORY
7. MISS AMERICA
8. POINSETTIA
9. RADIO
10. FLAMBEAU

These also do well: Dickson's Red; President Hoover; Charlotte Armstrong.

Although Blacksburg is a mountain plateau 2,200 feet above sea level, rose studies here suggest that basic results obtained would apply along the Virginia coast, where camellias grow beautifully out-of-doors.

ROSES IN TENNESSEE
Mrs. Horace N. Smith
Memphis, Tennessee

I find selecting my favorite ten roses quite a task because I always like best the last beautiful rose that I cut. In my list are several old roses, which bloom so well for me that I would not like a garden without them.

1. ETOILE DE HOLLANDE
2. CRIMSON GLORY
3. EDITOR MCFARLAND
4. MME. COCHET-COCHET
5. STERLING
6. KATHERINE T. MARSHALL
7. PINK PRINCESS
8. BETTY UPRICHARD
9. MRS. PIERRE S. DUPONT
10. MME. BUTTERFLY

Outstanding hardy climbers are Hercules (pink) and Thor (red).

ROSES IN TENNESSEE

MRS. ROBERT L. McREYNOLDS
Knoxville, Tennessee

1. PEACE
2. MIRANDY
3. GRANDE DUCHESSE
   CHARLOTTE
4. SONATA
5. MME. HENRI GUILLOT

6. SATURNIA
7. CRIMSON GLORY
8. PICTURE
9. CHARLOTTE ARMSTRONG
10. ECLIPSE

May I leave a word of advice for any one with limited space to plant some of these wonderful climbers?
Climbing Picture
Climbing Edith Nellie Perkins
Climbing Mme. Henri Guillot
Climbing Countess Vandal
Paul's Lemon Pillar (Frau Karl Druschki x Maréchal Niel)
Sunburst—buds lovely for corsages

ROSES IN NORTH CAROLINA

GLENN O. RANDALL
Professor of Horticulture,
State College of Agriculture & Engineering
Raleigh, North Carolina

1. ANGELS MATEU
2. ECLIPSE
3. EDITOR MCFARLAND
4. ETOILE DE HOLLANDE
5. KAISERIN AUGUSTE
   VIKTORIA

6. MME. COCHET-COCHET
7. PEACE
8. PRESIDENT MACIA
9. RADIO
10. RED RADIANCE

ROSES IN SOUTH CAROLINA

Mrs. Ellison S. McKissick
Greenville, South Carolina

So beautiful were the roses last season that it is difficult to say which ten are our favorites; however,

1. CRIMSON GLORY must be mentioned because she apparently liked good care and was glad to show her appreciation.

2. The old reliable, ETOILE DE HOLLANDE, sent forth an abundance of bloom all summer long.

3. And ECLIPSE, a veritable pumpkin shade, left off her blackspot to a greater degree than ever before.

4. COUNTESS VANDAL was a picture, particularly in the fall.

5. Every one was delighted with stately KATHERINE MARSHALL.

6. GOOD NEWS was ever a joy, supplying us with quantities of blooms.

7. We have gone from one white rose to another, always coming back to KAISERIN AUGUSTE VIKTORIA with her long pointed bud, slightly tinged with lemon.

8. DAINTY BESS possessed vigor as well as charm, and

9. ANGELS MATEU, exotic beauty, her foliage resembling waxed magnolia leaves.

10. Nor could we ever forget PEACE, having seen this exciting rose in three stages on one bush.

Author's Note

In this section of the Piedmont with its clay loam, Hybrid Teas grow to perfection. After a six weeks' disbudding period in midsummer, the fall bloom is magnificent.

ROSES IN GEORGIA
Hubert B. Owens
Head, Department of Landscape Architecture,
University of Georgia,
Athens, Georgia

1. CHARLOTTE ARMSTRONG
2. PICTURE
3. ETOILE DE HOLLANDE
4. ECLIPSE
5. LOUIS PHILIPPE—(Bengal) deep purplish red—good for hedges.
6. MADAM LOMBARD—Tea
7. BELLE OF PORTUGAL—2,000 gigantic pink buds on this rampant California climber! Early. A "natural" for the lower and middle South.
8. MARY WALLACE—hardy climber
9. YELLOW BANKSIA
10. PINOCCHIO—Floribunda

ROSES IN GEORGIA
A Composite List
Mrs. Aubrey Matthews, Mrs. J. H. O'Neill, and Others,
Rome, Georgia

1. ETOILE DE HOLLANDE
2. CRIMSON GLORY
3. CHARLES K. DOUGLAS
4. BRIARCLIFF
5. PICTURE
6. COUNTESS VANDAL
7. MRS. CHARLES BELL
8. SUNBURST—climber
9. CLIMBING COLUMBIA
10. KITTY KININMONTH—climber

ROSES IN GEORGIA
JAMES HYDE PORTER
Porterfield, Macon, Georgia

1. CHARLOTTE ARMSTRONG
2. PEACE
3. CRIMSON GLORY
4. CHARLES K. DOUGLAS
5. TEXAS CENTENNIAL
6. MME. COCHET-COCHET
7. ETOILE DE HOLLANDE
8. POINSETTIA
9. KAISERIN AUGUSTE VIKTORIA
10. ELIZABETH OF YORK

ROSES IN GEORGIA
MRS. THOMAS HOWELL SCOTT
Atlanta, Georgia

1. CRIMSON GLORY—always my favorite.
2. CHARLOTTE ARMSTRONG
3. ECLIPSE
4. ETOILE DE HOLLANDE

and all of the following climbers:

5. MERMAID
6. YELLOW BANKSIA
7. Climbing DAINTY BESS
8. Climbing COUNTESS VANDAL
9. RUTH ALEXANDER
10. DAYDREAM

ROSES IN GEORGIA
MRS. REGNALD MAXWELL,
Augusta, Georgia

1. MME. HENRI GUILLOT
2. ANGELS MATEU
3. COUNTESS VANDAL
4. MME. COCHET-COCHET
5. CALIFORNIA
6. R.M.S. QUEEN MARY
7. TREASURE ISLAND
8. CLIMBING SHOT SILK
9. SOEUR THERESE
10. PRINCESS MARINA

ROSES IN GEORGIA
Rodney S. Cohen,
Augusta, Georgia

While these are my favorite roses, they are not necessarily those I would recommend for purchase.

1. ANGELS MATEU	6. FAIENCE
2. MME. HENRI GUILLOT	7. KATHERINE T. MARSHALL
3. CHRISTOPHER STONE	8. MME. JOSEPH PERRAUD
4. COUNTESS VANDAL	9. CHARLOTTE ARMSTRONG
5. SATURNIA	10. SOEUR THERESE

I am also partial to Vesuvius and Texas Centennial.

ROSES IN GEORGIA
Jacob Lowrey,
Augusta, Georgia

1. SIERRA GLOW and
2. NUMA FAY (with me are absolute tops.)
3. PRESIDENT MACIA
4. COUNTESS VANDAL
5. ETOILE DE HOLLANDE
6. FEU PERNET-DUCHER
7. FAIENCE
8. MME. COCHET-COCHET
9. GAIETY
10. ECLIPSE

ROSES IN GEORGIA
William B. Jones,
Augusta, Georgia

1. MME. HENRI GUILLOT	7. GRANDE DUCHESSE
2. PEACE	CHARLOTTE
3. MRS. PIERRE S. DUPONT	8. HORACE MCFARLAND
4. CHARLOTTE ARMSTRONG	9. MARK SULLIVAN
5. ETOILE DE HOLLANDE	10. CLIMBING MRS. SAM
6. SOEUR THERESE	MCGREDY

ROSES IN GEORGIA
Mrs. William B. White,
Augusta, Georgia

1. MME. HENRI GUILLOT
2. CHARLOTTE ARMSTRONG
3. PEACE
4. MRS. SAM MCGREDY
5. THE DOCTOR
6. PORTADOWN FRAGRANCE
7. COUNTESS VANDAL
8. FAIENCE
9. ETOILE DE HOLLANDE
10. ECLIPSE

I love all roses—so how can I say which ten I like best? I wish to add: Lady Ashtown, Willowmere, Lady Alice Stanley, Angels Mateu, Mme. Cochet-Cochet.

ROSES IN GEORGIA
Mrs. George C. Baird,
Augusta, Georgia

1. MME. HENRI GUILLOT
2. PEACE
3. CLIMBING MRS. SAM MCGREDY
4. CLIMBING PICTURE
5. CHARLOTTE ARMSTRONG
6. CRIMSON GLORY
7. FASHION (Floribunda)
8. THE DOCTOR
9. SIERRA GLOW
10. ECLIPSE

ROSES IN GEORGIA
Andrew Prather,
Columbus, Georgia

All of these roses I find very hardy and prolific:

1. ECLIPSE
2. CHARLOTTE ARMSTRONG
3. PICTURE
4. CRIMSON GLORY
5. ETOILE DE HOLLANDE
6. DAINTY BESS
7. PEACE

Plant Pat. No. 129

MME. COCHET-COCHET
One of the winners in the Rose Poll

ROSES IN GEORGIA
Mrs. P. D. Fulwood,
Tifton, Georgia

1. ETOILE DE HOLLANDE
2. CRIMSON GLORY
3. PICTURE
4. EDITOR MCFARLAND
5. CECILE BRUNNER (Sweetheart)—Polyantha
6. ELSE POULSEN (Floribunda)
7. NEW DAWN—hardy climber—recurrent sport of Dr. Van Fleet.
8. PAUL'S SCARLET—hardy climber
9. LULU
10. PEACE

These and Radiance are a few of the roses most planted in Tifton.

ROSES IN GEORGIA
Mrs. Fred Scott,
Thomasville, Georgia

1. PINK RADIANCE
2. RED RADIANCE
3. MRS. CHARLES BELL
4. ETOILE DE HOLLANDE
5. EDITOR MCFARLAND
6. FRAU KARL DRUSCHKI (White American Beauty) Hybrid Perpetual
7. MADAM LOMBARD—Tea
8. MAMAN COCHET—Pink Tea
9. MRS. DUDLEY CROSS—Tea
10. WILLIAM R. SMITH—Tea

ROSES IN GEORGIA
Sam C. Hjort,
Thomasville, Georgia

1. MADAM LOMBARD—Bright Rose Pink Tea
2. PINK MAMAN COCHET—Tea
3. WHITE MAMAN COCHET—Tea

4. WILLIAM R. SMITH—Blush Pink Tea
5. MRS. DUDLEY CROSS—Light Yellow Tea
6. PINK RADIANCE
7. RED RADIANCE
8. MRS. CHARLES BELL
9. ETOILE DE HOLLANDE
10. EDITOR MCFARLAND

All of the Teas mentioned are long-lived, free bloomers, producing large flowers on stems suitable for cutting. Although my preference runs to the Tea rose, I find Eclipse the best yellow Hybrid Tea, Peace a wonderful new rose, and Crimson Glory very fine.

ROSES IN GEORGIA

A. J. NITZSCHKE,
Savannah, Georgia

These do well and are popular here:

1. CRIMSON GLORY
2. CHRISTOPHER STONE
3. ETOILE DE HOLLANDE
4. ECLIPSE
5. MME. JOSEPH PERRAUD
6. EDITOR MCFARLAND
7. PICTURE
8. CHARLOTTE ARMSTRONG
9. MME. COCHET-COCHET
10. SNOWBIRD

ROSES IN GEORGIA

MRS. DEWEY COOKE,
Savannah, Georgia

1. PRESIDENT MACIA
2. RAPTURE
3. MME. COCHET-COCHET
4. SIERRA GLOW
5. ETOILE DE HOLLANDE
6. CHRISTOPHER STONE
7. CHARLOTTE ARMSTRONG
8. MME. HENRI GUILLOT
9. ECLIPSE
10. MRS. PIERRE S. DUPONT

These ten favorites grow well in my garden.

ROSES IN ALABAMA
MRS. WALTER BROWN,
Birmingham, Alabama

1. ECLIPSE is always tops for me!
2. CRIMSON GLORY—best of all the reds.
3. WHITE BRIARCLIFF—finicky but dainty.
4. MME. COCHET-COCHET—with her golden heart is pretty first and last, particularly under artificial light.
5. CALIFORNIA doesn't bloom often, but when it does, what a rose!
6. MRS. PIERRE S. DUPONT—This sturdy lass will bloom for those who can't raise Eclipse.
7. PRESIDENT HOOVER—such a good old stand-by!
and my three toughies, who never let my rose bowls go empty, no matter if the weather is too wet or too dry:
8. MRS. CHARLES BELL
9. TALISMAN
10. YELLOW TALISMAN

If I might choose a dozen best, then I would include one good single, Dainty Bess, and one good Floribunda, Donald Prior.

ROSES IN ALABAMA
MRS. G. A. ROBINSON,
Cullman, Alabama

1. RED RADIANCE
2. ETOILE DE HOLLANDE
3. CRIMSON GLORY
4. SNOWBIRD
5. GOLDEN DAWN
6. EDITOR MCFARLAND
7. MARGARET MCGREDY
8. MAMAN COCHET—Tea
9. CECILE BRUNNER—Bush Polyantha (The Sweetheart Rose).
10. CECILE BRUNNER—climber.

IF I COULD HAVE JUST TEN ROSES

RALPH M. DASHER,

Florence, Alabama

Naming my ten favorite roses is somewhat similar to choosing just ten friends, forsaking all others. Although my team represents a choice from the heart, all are of vigorous growth, free flowering, and season-long performers even in the blasting heat of our summers.

1. CHARLOTTE ARMSTRONG—easily the finest rose in our garden.

2. CRIMSON GLORY—far superior to every other red rose or to almost any rose.

3. ECLIPSE—the best all-purpose yellow.

4. SIERRA GLOW—can be grown to five or six feet by proper pruning. Flowers last for days.

5. DEBONAIR—outstanding for the perfection of its yellow buds. This recent introduction surpasses its more highly publicized rivals.

6. NUMA FAY—has the edge on Good News, almost its twin.

7. THE DOCTOR—huge blooms of glowing pink. Fragrance detectable yards away.

8. MIRANDY—puts on its best performance in the heat of our long summer. Superbly fragrant, with large maroon buds and full blooms on a good plant.

9. SHOW GIRL—deep pink buds, sometimes breath-taking, open into exhibition blooms. Although color and fragrance are below that of The Doctor, the plant, itself, is one of the best.

10. PEACE—not up to its catalogue raves (no rose could be!) but when the hydrangea-size blooms contain sufficient yellow, it's superb.

ROSES IN MISSISSIPPI
Mrs. U. G. Flowers,
Vicksburg, Mississippi

1. CRIMSON GLORY—well named! It blooms constantly and seldom has blackspot.
2. ETOILE DE HOLLANDE and climbing Etoile de Hollande are excellent under all conditions.
3. CHRISTOPHER STONE
4. PEACE
5. EDITOR MCFARLAND—I advise disbudding for handsomest blooms.
6. MRS. CHARLES BELL
7. DAINTY BESS
8. MERMAID—a rank grower, needing plenty of space, is a constant bloomer from April till heavy frost. A splendid climber.
9. PRESIDENT MACIA
10. FOLKESTONE

ROSES IN MISSISSIPPI
Mrs. Mary S. Shook,
Ellisville, Mississippi

Yellows

1. MANDALAY
2. MME. MARIE CURIE
3. GOLDILOCKS—Floribunda

Reds

4. FLAMBEAU
5. RUBAIYAT
6. ETOILE DE HOLLANDE
7. CRIMSON GLORY—particularly the climbing form

Pinks
8. KATHERINE T. MARSHALL

Bi-Colors
9. MME. JOSEPH PERRAUD
10. COUNTESS VANDAL

The old varieties mentioned I have grown for eight years, the very new ones for three or four years as a test rose.

ROSES IN MISSISSIPPI
MRS. HARRIS BARKSDALE,
Jackson, Mississippi

1. CRIMSON GLORY
2. THE DOCTOR
3. ETOILE DE HOLLANDE
4. NUMA FAY or Good News
5. ECLIPSE
6. KOROVO
7. PICTURE
8. GAIETY
9. POINSETTIA
10. MME. JULES BOUCHE

THE NEW ORLEANS STORY
HARRY L. DAUNOY,
Garden Consultant,
New Orleans, Louisiana

I shall try to tell the New Orleans rose story very briefly. The early literature describes every cottage as being covered with Lamarque, Maréchal Niel, Cherokee, and other old-fashioned roses. All of these began to disappear about 1900, and had vanished fifteen years later. In 1930, the only roses seen in New Orleans were a few varieties like Louis Philippe and Radiance. Investigation disclosed that quite a change had taken place in the soil, and that it would be necessary to apply certain treatments to make roses grow. There was sufficient enthusiasm by 1939 to put on the first of our many successful rose shows.

I have selected ten Hybrid Teas, none of them new, which have succeeded here:

1. ETOILE DE HOLLANDE
2. CHRISTOPHER STONE
3. DAINTY BESS
4. SNOWBIRD
5. TEXAS CENTENNIAL
6. SUSAN LOUISE
7. PICTURE
8. COUNTESS VANDAL
9. SOEUR THERESE
10. KAISERIN AUGUSTE VIKTORIA

THE ROSE, A NEW ORLEANS FAVORITE

MARTA LAMAR

Garden Editor, the New Orleans TIMES-PICAYUNE

The rose is a New Orleans favorite. A census-taking of the front yards and back gardens, especially where there is room for only a few plants, reveals the rose in top position numerically. Tried-and-true Southern favorites, famous for their long life are:

1. TALISMAN (sunset colors)
2. KAISERIN AUGUSTE VIKTORIA (white) and
3. ETOILE DE HOLLANDE (red)

All three of these above thrive in climbing as well as bush form.

Varieties which, with brief periods of rest, will bloom almost year round in New Orleans, right through Christmas and the New Year, are:

4. RADIANCE, pink or red
5. CRIMSON GLORY
6. EDITOR MCFARLAND, a fragrant pink, and
7. MRS. B. R. CANT, a pink Tea

Other standbys include:

8. COLUMBIA, a pink beauty, especially hardy as climber (less so as bush) and

9. KOROVO, a healthy pink, which has for one of its parents the staunch, disease-resistant Etoile de Hollande.

10. Every one agrees that New Orleans would not be New Orleans in the spring without yellow and white BANKSIA.

Stressing old favorites is wise, but it is also fun to try some of the new rose creations presented by rosarians each year. Growing roses is an adventure, and to forego a new rose or so each January is like refusing to taste a delightful new drink offered, or to refrain from trying on all the new hats presented for your inspection.

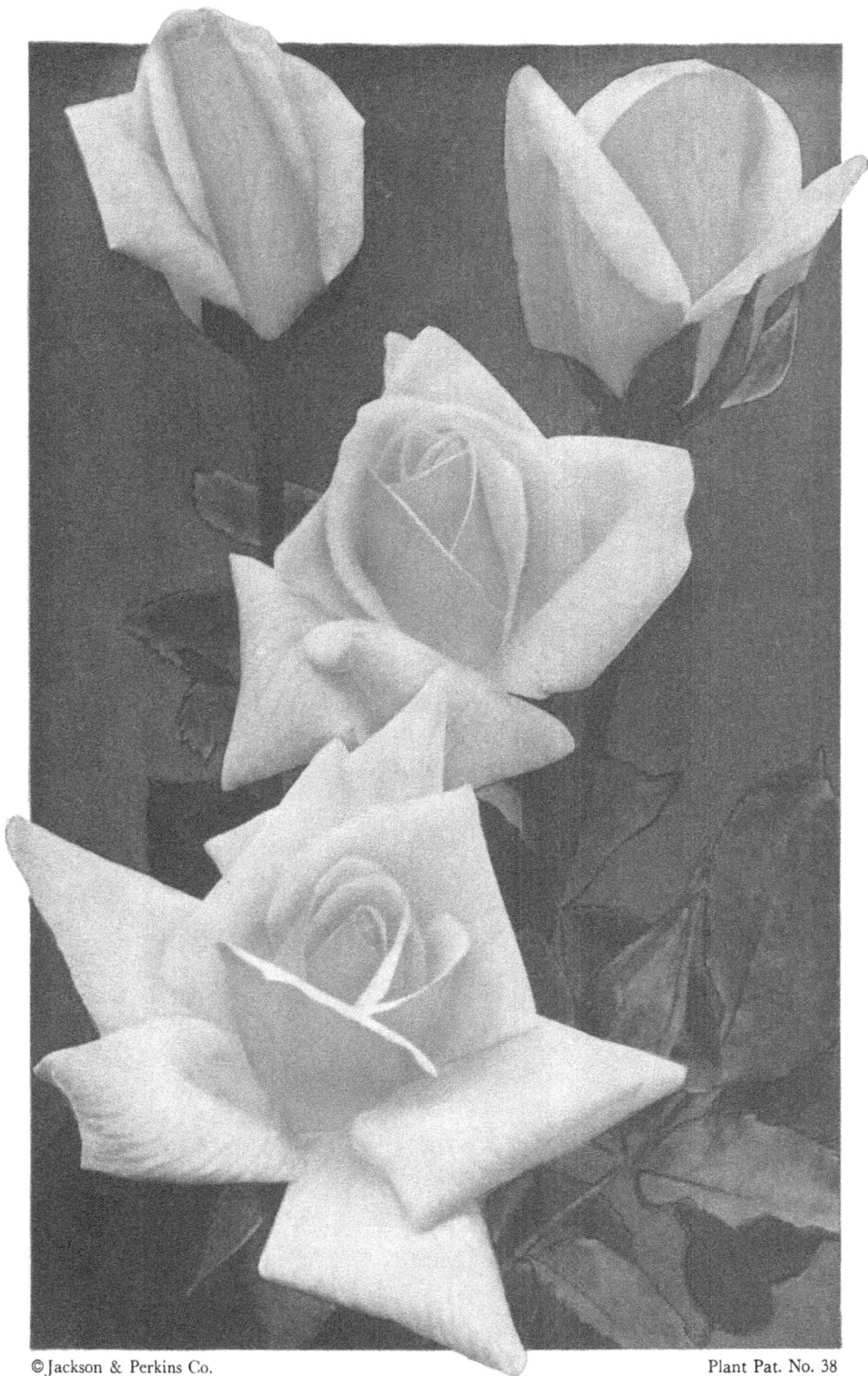

Plant Pat. No. 38

COUNTESS VANDAL
"This everblooming Rose is a moving picture in technicolor"

ᦄ 15 ᦅ

ROSEATE AXIOMS AND JINGLES *

Pot-pourri

THE EARLY ROSE order gets the pick of the crop.
Green thumbs are given a lot of credit that the back
deserves.

A pair of cotton gloves is a vital item of equipment.

Beginner's Luck has stolen many a Rose Show.

Visit the garden in the early morning, and enjoy the
roses at their peak of perfume.

There's nothing to equal a spot of blue in the garden to
set off the beauty of the roses. Have you tried: Shrub-like
Plumbago capensis; Bearded Iris, Shining Waters or Great
Lakes; Siberian Iris, Perry's Blue; or that little California
gem, *Dianella tasmanica?*

Types We All Know—Who Say Roses Won't Grow for Them

1. The humanitarian who boards the cat out at the Cat
Hospital when she goes away to the mountains in July, but
turns her roses over to a Yard Man who starts an overhead
sprinkler in late afternoon.

2. The flower arranger who thinks one rose with a long

---

* With respectful apology to *The Ancient Mariner, The Mikado, Mother
Goose, Alice in Wonderland,* and *The Charleston Almanack and Register.*

stem in the house is worth two on the bush. Pretty soon she won't have a bush.

3. The enthusiast who, hearing that a little clay is good for roses, decides that 100% clay will be better.

4. The energetic housekeeper who cultivates so deeply that she injures the fine feeder roots near the surface.

Planting Instructions

Roses grown in the shade are spindleshanks. They love sun two-thirds of the day.

Rose soil is what you make it.

SIMPLE ARITHMETIC: Proper soil preparation will multiply your bloom by four.

> The North Wind doth blow,
> We might even have snow,
> And what will the Rose Bush do then,
>   poor thing?
> New set in the ground, with a temporary
>   "mound,"
> 'Twill stay warm to blossom in spring,
>   sure thing!

> "Who killed that Rose Bush?"
> "I," said the Gardener.
> "I didn't plant on a 'mound,' and spread
>   the roots all around,
> I killed that Rose Bush!
> I also didn't 'tread,' that's why it's dead,
>   I'm really afraid
> That I killed that Rose Bush!
> Then I didn't water just as I ought to,
> I killed that Rose Bush!
> And after I was through, something else
>   I didn't do
> Was mound up the soil, it seemed too
>   much toil,
> I killed that Rose Bush!"

General Garden Care

A small dose of fertilizer administered regularly is better than a large dose at long intervals.

Leave liquid manure to the fellow who recommends it.

Everyone has heard the old adage: ROSES DON'T LIKE WET FEET.

The Sand Hills of Georgia version: ROSES DON'T LIKE DRY FEET.

As far as the roses are concerned, the best thing to do to a hackberry tree is to hack it down. Compromise on the second best course. Twice yearly cut out those underground, octopus tentacles before they strangle the life out of the rose roots.

Vitally Important Statistics (U. S. Department of Agriculture): On a given day at the end of a hot, dry week—
Temperature 1 ft. above soil level: 94°
Temperature top 2 inches in unmulched bed: 124°
Temperature top 2 inches in mulched bed: 84°
Comparison Proves!

> Day after day, day after day of drought
> And heat wave in addition,
> Arise from bed, you sleepy head,
> And gird up your ambition.

> Water, water every morn,
> From this duty do not shrink.
> Water, water every morn,
> Your roses need a drink!

> A mulch is such a useful thing!
> Why cultivate and till?
> It labor saves—great thanks be given!
> It also holds the rain from Heaven
> And cuts the water bill.

Rose bushes manufacture in their leaves 95% of their food, storing it in canes and roots. Heavy pruning robs the warehouse of last summer's hoard.

Spraying and Dusting

It's easier to prevent rose diseases than to cure them.

A wise gardener once said: Save the foliage and you save all.

Spring style forecast: The well-groomed Rose Bush will be becomingly clad in a Fermate raincoat this season.

When the Bugs invite their sisters and their cousins and their aunts to hold their Family Reunion in your garden, go after them with a spray gun!

A nicotine spray runs the aphids away,
Else a rotenone dust is an absolute "must."

In spring, when spraying the camellias with Volck, avoid wetting the nearby climbing Hybrid Teas, just recently sulphur-dusted.

In spraying, TIMING is of prime importance.

Climbers

PAGING CLIMBING MRS. SAM MCGREDY!

Roses that bloom in the spring, tra-la,
(It really makes very good sense)
Should also bloom in the fall, tra-la,
To be worthy of your picket fence!

CLIMBING KAISERIN AUGUSTE VIKTORIA

Mary had a climbing rose,
Its blossoms white as snow,
She sprayed and fertilized it well,
And how that rose did grow!

"Why does it bloom for Mary so?"
Her envious friends did sigh.
"Because," she said, "I care bestow,
Its roots are never dry.

Its horizontal arms outstretched
Absorb the morning light,
And full of buds, in spring and fall,
It is a lovely sight."

Let CLIMBING ETOILE DE HOLLANDE be the star in your garden crown. A trellis full of bloom at Thanksgiving is something to be thankful about.

Nomenclature

My roses belong to the International set,
Some of them French, and it hardly seems rational, yet
Others are British, even Spanish and Dutch,
Some Irish, American, German, and such.

Kaiserin Auguste Viktoria and Princess Marina,
The Grande Duchesse Charlotte, I never have seen a
Galaxy like Alice Stanley, the Lady,
Madame Henri Guillot, and plain Mrs. McGredy.

Lulu and Gipsy Lass—it's almost a scandal
The way they hobnob with young Countess Vandal.
But when quarrels arise and things come to grief,
General MacArthur needs help from the Chief.

"It's because Satan has entered this garden," I cry,
"The Reverend Page-Roberts must be stationed
     nearby.
I'll bolster his courage with Sister Therese,
Then throw out old Satan, and there I'll plant
     Peace!"

Now I ask in what realm has proud Mother Nature
A more intriguing and apt nomenclature?

Alice's Adventure in pH Land

At the end of the rose garden Alice saw the March Hare standing in a summer-house. He beckoned to her to enter, and there at his feet was a spring. Slowly turning on her heel, just like a compass, Alice read aloud an inscription encircling the ceiling:

> "A little learning is a dangerous thing,
> Drink deep or taste not the Pierian Spring."

"Oh," said Alice, "so this is the Pierian Spring! I had an idea that it was mythical like the Fountain of Youth. May I have a drink?" she asked.

"I wouldn't, if I were you," cautioned the March Hare. "The Queen did, and she's been a pHool ever since. She considers herself an authority on rose soil now, and calls herself the Queen of the Roses."

"Why doesn't she take a deep drink from the Spring?" sensibly inquired Alice.

"Tastes too bitter. Anyway," explained the March Hare, "she doesn't know she's a pHool. Nobody ever does. And it's lèse majesté to tell a queen that she's one. Do you like riddles?" he suddenly wanted to know. "And are you rather good at roses?"

"I like roses, and I'm rather good at riddles," Alice replied modestly.

"In that case," said the March Hare, taking a long breath, "try this one:

> "If rose foliage is the food factory for
>   the roots,
> And if—strong root systems produce
>   abundant foliage—
> Which is more important—
> The chicken or the egg?"

"Are you sure you didn't taste that spring, too?" queried Alice.

"Oh, no," answered the March Hare, "I was already mad!"

"Look at those funny thermometers poked in the ground beside every rose bush!" Alice exclaimed.

"That," said the March Hare, proudly extracting one, "is a pH-O-meter. The Mad Hatter invented it."

Alice gazed with interest at a stick, on which at the half-way mark was drawn the figure 7. Beneath, just like a problem in addition.

6.5
6.
5.5
5.
4.5 ran on down to the answer
ACIDOSIS

Likewise, on the opposite side of the stick, numerals steadily increasing in value ascended from 7 right on through 9.5 to CHLOROSIS. The painted "mercury," however, stopped dead on 7.

The March Hare continued, "The Queen's made the Hatter Head Gardener now. And here are his assistants, Tweedledum and Tweedledee." Those two gentlemen stepped forward and bowed stiffly.

Tweedledum became very conversational: "Because the Queen required daily tests, the Hatter saw that eventually he would send the entire garden in samples to the Soil Testing Service. Then the Queen would most certainly cut off his head. And what's the use of being Head Gardener without any head?"

Tweedledee added, "And unless the report was neutral, the Queen went into a rage. In self defense, the Hatter invented a soil meter which always reads 7."

"Very ingenious," commented Alice.

"Contrariwise," objected Tweedledee, "I call it smart. The Queen is happy, the roses bloom, and the Hatter keeps his head to wear his hat."

"Do you like poetry?" Tweedledee asked Alice.

"Ye-es, pretty well—some poetry," but Alice sounded doubtful.

"We know a poem," enticed Tweedledum, "that is very horticultural. The Hatter lets us recite it when the Queen's not around."

TWEEDLEDUM:

"Tell me what this pH stands for, with its little and
    big initial!
Will you make your explanation clear, but thor-
    oughly official?
With B.O. I am familiar, H_2S and T.N.T.,
But my I.Q.'s not sufficient for pH or Ph.D."

TWEEDLEDEE:

"This handy way to indicate if soil is sweet or sour,
Is a complicated subject to engross you by the hour.
A soil sample sent in to your Agricultural Station
Reveals its scientific hydrogen-Ion concentration.

"No matter if the soil reaction is a trifle acid,
Roses seem to like it, so you might as well stay placid,
Nor go into a panic if it's slightly alkaline,
For good soil that is ORGANIC will grow roses super-
    fine."

DIRECTIONS *for* ROSE CULTURE

Done by a Lady

(IN THE MANNER OF)

THE

CHARLESTON ALMANACK

AND

REGISTER

FOR THE ESPECIAL BENEFIT OF CHARLESTONIANS *but which without ſenſible Error may ſerve all the Provinces adjacent, even from Savannah in Georgia to Jameſtown in Virginia.*

January is a ſuitable month to plant Roſes, eſpecially the Noiſette-Tea Roſes, likewiſe Roſe-Trees.

It is very needfull to ſecure rich mellow Earth, when making a Roſe-Bed. Stable-Litter, ſpread thick and ſpaded in during the fall, is a good Expedient to forward the growth of the new plants, and will amply reward thy Labour.

Store Oak Aſhes from the Hearth in a proper veſſel with a lid. Sprinkle them in both ſpring and fall around the Roſes, ſcratch in lightly, and ſpeedily note the good effects thereof.

In order that foul weeds may not abound in the garden, apply Dung only in the laſt Quarter of the Moon.

Be on the watch for vexatious inſect Peſts, when they come abroad to do Miſchief. Make a bucketfull of Water ſudſy with ſuperior ſoft Soap; add a modicum of clarified Juice of Tobacco; and whiſk briſkly with a broom over the Roſes when Lice are bad. If ſorely afflicted, dip the ſtems into the Bucket.

Remember: plant thy Roſe-Buſhes well in winter— And gather ye Roſebuds in April and May.

The form and wording of the preceding page was suggested by *The Charleston Almanack and Register for the Year 1947*, published by The Historical Commission of Charleston, S. C. I am indebted to this source for much of the material employed.

INDEX

Acidosis, 87
Alabama, roses in, 75
Alfalfa leaf meal, 54
Ambassador, height of, 22; mentioned, 24
American Rose Society, address of, 61 n.; mentioned, 39, 61
Angels Mateu, in formal bed, 20; mentioned, 67, 68, 70, 71, 72
Annuals, in formal bed, 20
Aphids, description and treatment of, 40, 84; mentioned, 38. See also Spraying and dusting
Austrian Yellow (Fetid Rose), 5, 6
Azaleas, 8

Banksia, 5, 12, 13, 80
Barksdale, Mrs. Harris, on roses in Mississippi, 78
Bearded Iris, 8, 81
Bed, preparation of, 25-27; depth of, 25; drainage of, 26; rocks in, 26; fertilizer in, 26-27; topsoil in, 27. See also Rose bed
Belle of Portugal, 5, 69
Bengal. See Louis Philippe
Betty Prior, height of, 22; mentioned, 16
Betty Uprichard, 23, 66
Billy Boiler, 4
Blackspot, 5, 6, 16, 37, 38, 39, 49. See also Spraying and dusting
Bleeding-heart, 8
Bonaparte, Empress Josephine, 5
Bone meal, 54
Briarcliff, 69
Brown, Mrs. Walter, on roses in Alabama, 75
Bush roses, 15

California, 70, 75
Camellias, 84
Candytuft, 9
Cécile Brunner, height of, 23; mentioned, 73, 75
Charles K. Douglas, 66, 69, 70
Charlotte Armstrong, in formal bed, 19, 20; height of, 22; described, 76; mentioned, 15, 23, 24, 49, 65, 66, 67, 69, 70, 71, 72, 74
Cherokee, 5, 12, 13, 78
Chief, The, 23, 24, 85
Chlorosis, 87
Christopher Stone, climbing, 16; height of, 22; mentioned, 11, 16, 23, 24, 65, 71, 74, 77, 79
Chrysanthemum, 8, 9
Clay, 82
Climbers. See Hardy climbers; Tender climbers
Climbing Columbia, 69. See also Columbia
Climbing Countess Vandal, 67, 70. See also Countess Vandal
Climbing Dainty Bess, 70. See also Dainty Bess
Climbing Edith Nellie Perkins, 67
Climbing Etoile de Hollande, 16, 85. See also Etoile de Hollande
Climbing Hybrid Teas, 5, 11-13, 24, 51. See also Hybrid Teas
Climbing Kaiserin Auguste Viktoria, 84. See also Kaiserin Auguste Viktoria
Climbing Mme. Henri Guillot, 67. See also Mme. Henri Guillot
Climbing Mrs. Sam McGredy, 71, 72, 84. See also Mrs. Sam McGredy

Mme. Marie Curie, 77

Mallerin, Charles, on fertilizer for rose bed, 55-56; tribute to, 65

Maman Cochet, 73, 75

Mandalay, 77

Manure, cow, 53

Maréchal Niel, 5, 67, 78

Margaret McGredy, 75

Margo Koster, height of, 23; mentioned, 15

Mark Sullivan, 23, 24, 71

Mary Wallace, 69

Massey, Dr. L. M., plant pathologist, 61

Matthews, Mrs. Aubrey, on roses in Georgia, 69

Maxwell, Mrs. R., on roses in Georgia, 70

Mealy bugs, description and treatment of, 41-42

Meilland, Francis, 65

Mermaid, described, 77; mentioned, 4, 70

Midge, description and treatment of, 41

Mildew, 37-38. *See also* Spraying and dusting

Mirandy, described, 76; mentioned, 67

Miss America, 66

Mississippi, roses in, 77-78

Moats, 53

Moderate growers, 22

Mrs. B. R. Cant, 79

Mrs. Charles Bell, height of, 22; mentioned, 65, 69, 73, 74, 75, 77

Mrs. Dudley Cross, 73, 74

Mrs. Edward Laxton, height of, 22; mentioned, 24

Mrs. Pierre S. duPont, height of, 22; mentioned, 23, 66, 71, 74, 75

Mrs. Pierre S. duPont III, chrysanthemum, 8

Mrs. Sam McGredy, 11, 12, 15, 23, 24, 72, 85. *See also* Climbing Mrs. Sam McGredy

Mulch, 46-47, 83

Multiflora japonica, understock, 14 n., 56

Muriate of potash, 55

Neige Parfum, 24

Nematode, description and treatment of, 42

New Dawn, 12, 73

New Orleans, rose cultivation in, 78-80

New Yorker, height of, 22

Nicolas, Dr. J. H., hybridizer, 1, 26, 57, 64, 65

Nitrogen, 54

Nitzschke, A. J., on roses in Georgia, 74

Nocturne, height of, 22; mentioned, 23, 24

Noisette, 5

Nomenclature, of roses, 85

North Carolina, roses in, 67

Numa Fay, described, 76; mentioned, 71, 78

Odorata, understock, 57

O'Neill, Mrs. J. H., on roses in Georgia, 69

Ophiopogon, 9

Owens, Hubert B., on roses in Georgia, 69

Pansies, 8

Paul Neyron, 3

Paul's Lemon Pillar, 4, 67

Paul's Scarlet, 4, 73

Peace, in formal bed, 19, 20; height of, 22; described, 76; mentioned, 17, 23, 24, 49, 62, 65, 67, 68, 70, 71, 72, 73, 74, 77, 85

Peachblow, 24

Peat moss, 53

Pedrálbes, height of, 22; mentioned, 15, 23, 24

Perle d'Or, height of, 23

Pernet-Ducher, hybridizer, 5, 15

Pernetiana, 5

Perry's Blue, 81

Persian Yellow, 5

pH, defined, 54 n.; in rose cultivation, 57-59, 86-88

Phlox divaricata, 12

Phosphoric acid, 54

Picture, care of, 12; in formal bed, 19, 20; height of, 22; mentioned, 11, 23, 24, 65, 67, 69, 72, 73, 74, 78, 79. *See also* Climbing Picture

www.ingramcontent.com/pod-product-compliance
Lightning Source LLC
Chambersburg PA
CBHW030654270326
41929CB00007B/366